Introduction
to
MySQL

Shantanu Oak

Introduction
to
MySQL

Shantanu Oak

SHROFF PUBLISHERS & DISTRIBUTORS PVT. LTD.
Mumbai   Bangalore   Chennai   Kolkata   New Delhi

Introduction to MySQL
By *Shantanu Oak*

Copyright © 2005, Shantanu Oak

First Edition: November 2005
ISBN: 81-7366-463-3

Published by **Shroff Publishers & Distributors Pvt. Ltd.** C-103, T.T.C. Industrial Area, M.I.D.C., Pawane, Navi Mumbai - 400 701. Tel.: (91-22) 2763 4290 Fax: 2768 3337 E-mail:spdorders@shroffpublishers.com Printed at Decora Printers, Andheri, Mumbai.

Table of Contents

SQL

- SQL stands for Structured Query Language
- Dr. E. F. Ted Codd who worked for IBM described a relational model for database in 1970.
- In the year 92 ANSI (American National Standards Institute) the apex body, standardized most of the basic syntax.
- Its called SQL 92 and supported by most of the databases like oracle, mysql, sybase etc.

Why MySQL?

- Cost – Free!
- Support – Online tutorials, forums (devshed.com), mailing list (lists.mysql.com)
- Speed – One of the fastest databases available.
- Functionality – supports most of ANSI SQL commands.
- Ease of use – No need of training/ retraining.
- Portability – easily import/ export from excel or other databases.
- Scalable – Useful for both, small as well as large tables having millions of records.
- Collaboration – selectively grant or revoke permissions to users.

DDL and DML

- DDL (Data Definition Language) refers to the Create, alter and drop Table statements
- DML (Data Manipulation Language) refers to the Select, Insert, Update and Delete statements
  - o DQL (Data Query Language) refers to the Select statements

Table Types: myISAM and InnoDB

MyISAM does table level locking, while InnoDB does row level locking.

In addition to foreign keys, InnoDB offers transaction support, which is absolutely critical when dealing with larger applications.

Speed does suffer though because all this Foreign Key / Transaction stuff takes lots of overhead.

Table Type: Merge Table

- A MERGE table is a collection of identical MyISAM tables that can be used as one.
- Identical means that all tables have identical column and index information.

- CREATE TABLE mumbai (first_name VARCHAR(30), amount INT(10)) TYPE=MyISAM

- CREATE TABLE delhi (first_name VARCHAR(30), amount INT(10)) TYPE=MyISAM

- CREATE TABLE total (first_name VARCHAR(30), amount INT(10)) TYPE=MERGE UNION=(mumbai,delhi)

Views

(Mysql 5.0+)

CREATE VIEW view_name AS SELECT column_list... FROM table_name

DROP VIEW [IF EXISTS] view_name, view_name ....

SELECT VIEW_DEFINITION FROM information_schema.views WHERE TABLE_NAME = 'view_name'

Views are nothing but results of SQL queries saved as a separate table that does automatically gets updated whenever you update the original table. View creation makes no copy of the data, it's simply storing the SQL.

- Different users can be given access to the view but not the underlying table. It will be useful for the people who want to run reports against the data but don't have the experience with SQL.

- You can create the new view based on the existing view.
- It's possible to use niladic functions such as CURRENT_USER, CURRENT_TIME within views.
- Even if the view was created using select *, the view definition shows that the view is stored with the column names listed rather than storing the select *.

CREATE VIEW v_emp_detail AS SELECT emp_id, emp_name, description, salary FROM emps e, dept d WHERE e.dept_id = d.dept_id

User Variables

- The ability to set variables in a statement with the : = assignment operator.
- Variables hold single values. If you assign a value to a variable using a statement that returns multiple rows, the value from the last row is used.
- User variables are set for the duration of the thread.
- In the vast majority of cases you'd use a programming language to do this sort of thing.

- Mysql variables can be useful when working on the Mysql command line.
- If no records are returned, the user variable will not be set for that statement and the variable retains its previous value, if any.
- Variables are case sensitive
- Variables are a Mysql-specific extension.
- SELECT @m := MAX(marks) FROM result;
- SET @testsum := 4+7;
- The value of a variable is set with the SET statement or in a SELECT statement with :=

```
SET @startdate='some_start_date',
@enddate='some_end_date'

SELECT @torem:=COUNT(*) FROM membros;

SELECT @numdistinct := COUNT(DISTINCT field)
FROM table1 WHERE field <> 0;
SELECT @torem @numdistinct;
```

Alias

A select expression may be declared as an alias using AS. The alias is used as the expression's column name and can be used with order by or having clauses. For e.g.

```
SELECT CONCAT (last_name,' ', first_name) AS
full_name
FROM mytable
ORDER BY full_name
```

A table name can have a shorter name for reference using AS. You can omit the AS word and still use aliasing. For e.g.

```
SELECT COUNT(B.Booking_ID), U.User_Location
FROM Users U
LEFT OUTER JOIN Bookings B
ON U.User_ID = B.Rep_ID AND B.Project_ID = '10'
GROUP BY(U.User_Location)
```

Aliasing plays a crucial role while you are using self joins. For e.g. people table has been referred to as p and c aliases!

```
SELECT p.name as parent, c.name as child,
MIN((TO_DAYS(NOW())-TO_DAYS(c.dob))/365) as minage
FROM people as p
LEFT JOIN people as c
ON p.name=c.parent WHERE c.name IS NOT NULL
GROUP BY parent HAVING minage > 50 ORDER BY p.dob;
```

explain

When you precede a SELECT statement with the keyword EXPLAIN, MySQL explains how it would process the SELECT, providing information about how tables are joined and in which order.

explain select * from favorites where RECNO = 2

table	type	possible_keys	key	key_len	ref	rows
favorites	const	PRIMARY	PRIMARY	4	const	1

The output from EXPLAIN shows ALL in the type column when MySQL uses a table scan to resolve a query. The possible types are, from best to worst: system, const, eq_ref, ref, range, index and ALL.

Only index in the "Extra" column indicates that information will be retrieved from index file without using the data file.

DESCRIBE provides information about a table's columns. It is a shortcut for SHOW COLUMNS FROM.

DESCRIBE students;

select * from list

ID	Name	Surname	FlatHave	FlatWant
1	Shantanu	Oak	Goregaon	
2	Shantanu	Oak	Andheri	
3	Shantanu	Oak		Dadar
4	Ram	Joshi		Goregaon
5	Shyam	Sharma		Andheri
6	Ram	Naik	Sion	
7	Samir	Shah	Parle	
8	Ram	Joshi	Dadar	
9	Shyam	Sharma	Dadar	

Exercise I

1. Who has a flat in "Goreagon" and who wants to buy one?
2. Who has a flat in "Parle" and who wants to buy one?
3. Where does "Shantanu Oak" own the flats and where does he want to buy one?
4. How many entries have been recorded so far?
5. How many flats are there for sale?

6. What are the names of our clients?

7. How many clients do we have?

8. List the customers whose name start with "S"?

9. Rearrange the list Alphabetically sorted.

Answers to exercise I

1. select * from list where FlatHave = "Goregaon" or FlatWant = "Goregaon"

2. select * from list where FlatHave = "Parle" or FlatWant = "Parle"

3. select * from list where Name = "Shantanu" and Surname = "Oak"

4. select count(*) from list

5. select count(FlatHave) from list where FlatHave is not null

6. select distinct Name, Surname from list

7. select count(distinct Name, surname) from list

8. select * from list where Name like "S%"

9. select Surname, Name, FlatHave, FlatWant from list order by Surname

---

select * from grades

ID	Name	Math	Physics	Literature
1	John	68	37	54
2	Jim	96	89	92
3	Bill	65	12	57
4	Jeri	69	25	82

Exercise II

1. A list of all students who scored over 90 in their math paper?

2. More than 85 marks in all the subjects?

3. Declare Results: Print the results of all students with result column.

4. Find out total marks of all the students?

5. What are the average marks of the students?

6. What are the minimum marks in Maths?

7. What are the maximum marks in Maths?

8. Who got the highest marks in Maths?

Answers to exercise II

1. SELECT * FROM grades WHERE math > 90

2. SELECT name FROM grades WHERE math > 85 AND physics > 85 AND literature > 85

3. SELECT *, IF((math <= 35 OR physics <= 35 OR literature <= 35), 'fail', 'pass') AS result FROM grades ORDER BY result DESC

4. SELECT name, math+physics+literature AS total FROM grades

5. SELECT AVG(math), AVG(physics), AVG(literature) FROM grades

6. SELECT MIN(math) FROM grades

7. SELECT MAX(math) FROM grades

8. SELECT * FROM grades ORDER BY math DESC LIMIT 1

select

select syntax is as follows:

*select ***
FROM table
WHERE condition

In and not in

SELECT id
FROM stats
WHERE position IN ('Manager', 'Staff')

SELECT ownerid, 'is in both orders & antiques'
FROM orders, antiques WHERE ownerid = buyerid UNION
SELECT buyerid, 'is in antiques only'
FROM antiques WHERE buyerid NOT IN (SELECT
ownerid FROM orders);

Exists & All

(Mysql 4+)

SELECT ownerfirstname, ownerlastname
FROM owner
WHERE EXISTS (SELECT * FROM antiques
WHERE item = 'chair')

SELECT buyerid, item
FROM antiques
WHERE price = ALL (SELECT price FROM antiques)

Union and Union All

(Mysql 4+)

```
SELECT * FROM english
UNION ALL
SELECT * FROM hindi
```

All the records from both the tables will be returned.
UNION = UNION DISTINCT
If you type only UNION, then it is considered that you are asking for distinct records.
If you want all records, you have to say, UNION ALL
The word distinct will be silently used if you don't add "ALL" next to union statement.

```
SELECT word FROM word_table WHERE id = 1
UNION
SELECT word FROM word_table WHERE id = 2
```

```
(SELECT magazine FROM pages)
UNION DISTINCT
(SELECT magazine FROM pdflog)
ORDER BY magazine
```

```
(SELECT ID_ENTRY FROM table WHERE ID_AGE = 1)
UNION DISTINCT
(SELECT ID_ENTRY FROM table WHERE ID_AGE=2)
```

Joins

The Most important aspect of SQL is it's relational features. You can query, compare and calculate two different tables having entirely different structure. In the following example a student is trying to learn what the numbers are called in hindi.

select * from english		select * from hindi	
Tag	Inenglish	Tag	Inhindi
1	One	2	Do
2	Two	3	Teen
3	Three	4	Char

Cartesian join

A Cartesian join is when you join every row of one table to every row of another table.

select * from english, hindi

Tag	Inenglish	Tag	Inhindi
1	One	2	Do
2	Two	2	Do
3	Three	2	Do
1	One	3	Teen
2	Two	3	Teen
3	Three	3	Teen
1	One	4	Char
2	Two	4	Char
3	Three	4	Char

Inner Join

```
SELECT hindi.Tag, english.Inenglish, hindi.Inhindi
FROM english, hindi
WHERE english.Tag = hindi.Tag
```

Tag	Inenglish	Inhindi
2	Two	Do
3	Three	Teen

You can also write the same query as...
```
SELECT hindi.Tag, english.Inenglish, hindi.Inhindi
FROM english INNER JOIN hindi
ON english.Tag = hindi.Tag
```

Natural Joins
(Mysql 4+)

The following statement will display the same results because the column called 'Tag' is present in both tables.

```
SELECT hindi.tag, hindi.Inhindi, english.Inenglish
FROM hindi NATURAL JOIN english
```

Outer Joins

Tag	Inenglish	Tag	Inhindi
1	**One**		
2	Two	2	Do
3	Three	3	Teen
		4	**Char**

Left Outer Join

The syntax is as follows:
SELECT field1, field2 FROM table1 LEFT JOIN table2 ON field1=field2

```
SELECT e.Inenglish as English, e.Tag, '—no row—' as Hindi
FROM english AS e LEFT JOIN hindi AS h
ON e.Tag=h.Tag
WHERE h.Inhindi IS NULL
```

English	tag	Hindi
One	1	—no row—

Right Outer Join

```
SELECT '—no row—' AS English, h.tag, h.lnhindi AS
Hindi
FROM english AS e RIGHT JOIN hindi AS h
ON e.Tag=h.Tag
WHERE e.lnenglish IS NULL
```

English	tag	Hindi
—no row—	4	Char

- Make sure that you have the same name and same data type in both tables.

- The keywords LEFT and RIGHT are not absolute, they only operate within the context of the given statement: we can reverse the order of the tables and reverse the keywords, and the result would be the same.

- If the type of join is not specified as inner or outer then it will be executed as an INNER JOIN.

Subqueries
(Mysql 4.1+)

- SQL subqueries let you use the results of one query as part of another query.

- Subqueries are often natural ways of writing a statement.

- Let you break a query into pieces and assemble it.

- Allow some queries that otherwise can't be constructed. Without using a subquery, you have to do it in two steps.

- Subqueries generally appear as part of the WHERE (or HAVING) clause.

- Only one field can be in the subquery SELECT. It means Subquery can only produce a single column of data as its result.

- ORDER BY is not allowed; it would not make sense.

- Usually refer to name of a main table column in the subquery.

- This defines the current row of the main table for which the subquery is being run. This is called an outer reference.

For e.g. If RepOffice= OfficeNbr from Offices table, list the offices where the sales quota for the office exceeds the average of individual salespersons' quotas

SELECT City FROM Offices WHERE Target > ???

??? is the sum of the quotas of the salespeople, i.e.

```
SELECT AVG(Quota)
FROM SalesReps
WHERE RepOffice = OfficeNbr
```

We combine these to get
```
SELECT City FROM Offices
WHERE Target > (SELECT AVG(Quota) FROM SalesReps
WHERE RepOffice = OfficeNbr)
```

Trigger
(Mysql 5.0+)

To create a trigger the code needs to be entered into the MySQL command line.

You can have only one trigger per type per table.

```
CREATE TRIGGER bi_emps_fer BEFORE
INSERT ON emps FOR EACH ROW

SET NEW.emp_name :=
REVERSE(NEW.emp_name)
```

Multi - line code needs to be enclosed within a BEGIN and END.
Unlike procedures or functions we cannot invoke triggers manually, they must be called as a result of the relevant table action.

To fire the trigger a record needs to be inserted into the relevant table.

```
INSERT INTO emps (emp_id,emp_name) VALUES
(4,'dave')
```

insert

The syntax is as follows:
insert into TableName (Column1, Column2, Column3)
values (value1, value2, value3)

insert into TableName
values (value1, value2, value3)

insert into TableName
values (value1, value2, value3), (value4, value5, value6)

INSERT INTO table1(feld1, field2)
SELECT field1, field2
FROM table2

Examples...

INSERT INTO antiques VALUES (21, 01, 'Ottoman', 200.00);
INSERT INTO antiques (buyerid, sellerid, item)
VALUES (01, 21, 'Ottoman');

You can also insert records 'selected' from other table.

INSERT INTO World_Events SELECT * FROM National_Events

---

update

The syntax is...

UPDATE <table>
SET <field> = <newvalue> where <criteria>

Examples...

```
UPDATE owner SET ownerfirstname = 'John'
WHERE ownerid = (SELECT buyerid
FROM antiques WHERE item = 'Bookcase');
```

```
UPDATE antiques SET price = 500.00
WHERE item = 'Chair';
```

```
UPDATE order SET discount=discount * 1.05
```

```
UPDATE tbl1 JOIN tbl2 ON tbl1.ID = tbl2.ID
SET tbl1.col1 = tbl1.col1 + 1
WHERE tbl2.status='Active'
```

```
UPDATE tbl SET names = REPLACE(names, 'aaa', 'zzz')
```

```
UPDATE products_categories AS pc
INNER JOIN products AS p ON pc.prod_id = p.id
SET pc.prod_sequential_id = p.sequential_id
```

```
UPDATE table_name SET col_name =
REPLACE(col_name, 'host.domain.com',
'host2.domain.com')
```

delete

The syntax is...
DELETE FROM table
WHERE <criteria>

Example:
DELETE FROM antiques
WHERE item = 'Ottoman'

- If you don't use a WHERE clause with DELETE, all records will be deleted.

- TRUNCATE will do the same quickly by dropping and re-creating the table. But the auto incremented column will be reset.

- DELETE with a condition will inform you how many rows have been removed, but TRUNCATE won't

DELETE FROM table1 WHERE 1 = 1
TRUNCATE table1

drop

DROP TABLE products

will completely delete the records as well as the columns.

---

alter

alter table command can be used when you want to add / delete the columns or change the data type.

```
ALTER TABLE awards
ADD COLUMN AwardCode int(2)

ALTER TABLE awards
ALTER COLUMN AwardCode VARCHAR(2) NOT NULL

ALTER TABLE awards
MODIFY AwardCode VARCHAR(2) NOT NULL

ALTER TABLE awards
DROP COLUMN AwardCode
```

create

Create table syntax is:
CREATE TABLE tablename (FieldName1 DataType, FieldName2 DataType)

The rows returned by the "select" query can be saved as a new table. The datatype will be the same as the old table. For e.g.

```
CREATE TABLE LearnHindi
SELECT english.tag, english.Inenglish AS english,
hindi.Inhindi AS hindi
FROM english, hindi
WHERE english.tag = hindi.tag
```

Grants

GRANT <privileges> ON <database>
TO <user> [IDENTIFIED BY <password>
WITH GRANT OPTION]

GRANT ALL PRIVILEGES ON vworks.*
TO newuser@localhost IDENTIFIED BY
'newpassword';

GRANT SELECT, INSERT, UPDATE,
DELETE ON vworks.* TO newuser@localhost
IDENTIFIED BY 'newpassword';

GRANT ALL PRIVILEGES ON vworks.*
TO newuser@192.168.0.2 IDENTIFIED BY
'newpassword';

GRANT ALL PRIVILEGES ON vworks.*
TO newuser@'%' IDENTIFIED BY
'newpassword';

GRANT ALL PRIVILEGES ON vworks.*
TO newuser@192.168.0.2;

GRANT ALL PRIVILEGES ON vworks.*
TO newuser@localhost IDENTIFIED BY
'newpassword' WITH GRANT OPTION;

GRANT SELECT, INSERT, UPDATE,
DELETE ON vworks.* TO friend@localhost
IDENTIFIED BY 'friendpass';

Revoke Privileges

Revoking privileges is almost identical to granting them as you simply substitute REVOKE.... FROM for GRANT....TO and omit any passwords or other options.

For example to REVOKE the privileges assigned to a user called 'badvworks':

REVOKE ALL PRIVILEGES ON vworks.* FROM badvworks@localhost;

Or just to remove UPDATE, INSERT and DELETE privileges to that data cannot be changed.

REVOKE INSERT,UPDATE,DELETE ON vworks.* FROM badvworks@localhost;

Order matters for GRANTs and REVOKEs. Last one governs.

Data Types

varchar(n)

VARCHAR is shorthand for CHARACTER VARYING. 'n' represents the maximum column length (upto 255 characters) char(n) is similar to varchar(n) with the only difference that char will occupy fixed length of space in the database whereas varchar will need the space to store the actual text. For example, a VARCHAR(10) column can hold a string with a maximum length of 10 characters. The actual storage required is the length of the string (L), plus 1 byte to record the length of the string.

For the string 'abcd', L is 4 and the storage requirement is 5 bytes.

text

A BLOB or TEXT column with a maximum length of 65,535 characters.

integer(n)

Specifying an n value has no effect whatsoever. Regardless of a supplied value for n, maximum (unsigned) value stored is 429 crores.

Integer Data type, by default allows negative values. If you want to enter only positive numbers, add the "UNSIGNED" keyword next to it.

decimal(n,m)

decimal(4,2) means numbers upto 99.99 (and NOT 9999.99 as you may expect) can be saved. Four digits with the last 2 reserved for decimal.

date

Out of the three types DATE, DATETIME, and TIMESTAMP, the DATE type is used when you need only a date value, without a time part.

MySQL retrieves and displays DATE values in 'YYYY-MM-DD' format.

The DATETIME type is used when you need values that contain both date and time information.

Set and enum

A SET datatype can hold any number of strings from a predefined list of strings specified during table creation. The SET datatype is similar to the ENUM datatype in that they both work with predefined sets of strings, but where the ENUM datatype restricts you to a single member of the set of predefined strings, the SET datatype allows you to store any of the values together, from none to all of them.

Date and time

```
SELECT * FROM mydatetest
WHERE datetimecol >= (DATE_SUB(CURDATE(), INTERVAL 1
YEAR))
```

```sql
AND datetimecol < DATE_ADD((DATE_SUB(CURDATE(),
INTERVAL 1 YEAR)), INTERVAL 1 DAY ;

SELECT IF(DAYOFMONTH(CURDATE()) <= 15,
DATE_FORMAT(CURDATE(), '%Y-%m-15'),
DATE_FORMAT(CURDATE() + INTERVAL 1
MONTH, '%Y-%m-15')) AS next15
FROM table;

SELECT YEAR('2002-05-10'), MONTH('2002-05-10'),
DAYOFMONTH('2002-05-10')

SELECT PurchaseDate FROM mytable WHERE
YEAR(PurchaseDate) <= YEAR(CURDATE())

SELECT * FROM mytable
WHERE start_time >= '2004-06-01 10:00:00' AND
end_time <= '2004-06-03 18:00:00'

SELECT * FROM t1
WHERE DATE_FORMAT(datetime_column, '%T')
BETWEEN '18:00:00' AND '19:00:00'

SELECT Start_time, End_time FROM mytable
WHERE Start_time >= NOW() - INTERVAL 4 HOUR
```

Optimize

Optimize where clause by using "column operator constant"

(e.g. 'birthdate' < NOW() - INTERVAL 16 YEAR).

This is a lot faster than calculating the expression for each record in the table (e.g. 'birthdate' + INTERVAL 16 YEAR < NOW())

There is no need to "fill in" the empty in auto numbered column since gaps in your sequence numbers are a normal consequence of having an active database.

Syntax

When you use DATE_FORMAT(), if I have a space character between DATE_FORMAT and the opening bracket I get an error.

Try writing it like:

SELECT DATE_FORMAT("20040601123456", '%Y-%m-%d');

You can't use a value calculated in the SELECT clause as a constraint in the WHERE clause (its a chicken & egg problem); the WHERE clause is what determines the values in the SELECT clause. What you want is the HAVING clause which is applied *after* all matching rows have been found.

Dealing with NULL

The function 'COALESCE' can simplify working with null values.

for example, to avoid showing null values by treating null as zero, you can type:

```
SELECT COALESCE(colname,0) FROM mytable WHERE COALESCE(colname,0) > 1;
```

In a date field, to treat NULL as the current date:

```
ORDER BY
(coalesce(TO_DAYS(date),TO_DAYS(CURDATE())))-
TO_DAYS(CURDATE()))
```

There is no product(column) function just like sum(column). The following code can be used.

```
exp(sum(log(coalesce(*the field you want to multiply*,1))))
```

The coalesce() function is there to guard against trying to calculate the logarithm of a null value and may be optional depending on your circumstances.

```
SELECT t4.gene_name, COALESCE(g2d.score,0),
COALESCE(dgp.score,0), COALESCE(pocus.score,0)
FROM t4
LEFT JOIN g2d ON t4.gene_name=g2d.gene_name
LEFT JOIN dgp ON t4.gene_name=dgp.gene_name
LEFT JOIN pocus ON t4.gene_name=pocus.gene_name;
```

Use of IFNULL() in your SELECT statement is to make the NULL any value you wish.

IFNULL(expr1,expr2)
If expr1 is not NULL, IFNULL() returns expr1, else it returns expr2.
IFNULL() returns a numeric or string value, depending on the context in which it is used:

```
mysql> SELECT IFNULL(1,0);
-> 1
mysql> SELECT IFNULL(NULL,10);
-> 10
mysql> SELECT IFNULL(1/0,10);
-> 10
mysql> SELECT IFNULL(1/0,'yes');
-> 'yes'
```

If you want to have NULL values presented last when doing an ORDER BY, try this:

```
SELECT * FROM my_table ORDER BY
ISNULL(field), field [ ASC | DESC ]
```

Bugs

Long texts are chopped to the correct size, not denied. If you have declared a column as INT instead of BIGINT, then mysql will silently convert a value to "2147483647" if it is greater than that.

Like Group by, Having can be used with an aggregate function - Avg(), Count(), Count (Distinct), Max(), Min(), or Sum() even if the respective column is not selected.

FULLTEXT Index on InnoDB tables are not supported.

slow index DROP and CREATE is a top complaint among MySQL users. Therefore you have to disable keys and not drop using IGNORE INDEX

Insert a NULL value in a NOT NULL field and the query gets executed. In short, you can't force NOT NULL...

Normalization

Normalization is the process of removing redundant data from your tables in order to improve storage efficiency, data integrity and scalability.

First, Second and Third Normal forms

1. Each column must contain only one value (atomic or indivisible)

2. All columns whose values are the same across multiple rows must be turned into their own table and related back. (Primary and Foreign Keys)

3. Every non-key column is dependent upon the Primary Key.

Need for Normalization of data

- Avoid repetition
- Save space - Portable: transferring or backing up the data should be easy.
- Easy to maintain data
- "Divide and Rule" - Divide the data in it's logical order
- Scalability should not be a problem for a normalized database.

This improvement is balanced against an increase in complexity and potential performance losses from the joining of the normalized tables at query-time.

Reserved Words

Difficult Column Names, Like 'DATE' — use backtick. If using "date" as a column name, enclose it in backticks ` as follows:

```
CREATE TABLE IF NOT EXISTS stocks (
pkey int NOT NULL auto_increment,
'date' date,
ticker varchar(5),
open decimal (9,2),
high decimal (9,2),
low decimal (9,2),
close decimal (9,2),
volume int,
timeEnter timestamp(14),
PRIMARY KEY (pkey)   ) ;
```

Replace and ignore

REPLACE works exactly like INSERT, except that if
an old record in the table has the same value as a
new record for a PRIMARY KEY or a UNIQUE index,
the old record is deleted before the new record is
inserted.

With IGNORE, invalid values are adjusted to the
closest values and inserted; warnings are produced
but the statement does not abort.

Prior to MySQL 4.0.1, INSERT ... SELECT implicitly
operates in IGNORE mode. As of MySQL 4.0.1,
specify IGNORE explicitly to ignore records that would
cause duplicate-key violations.

Finding Duplicates

```
SELECT Vendor, ID, Count(1) as dupes
FROM table_name
GROUP BY Vendor, ID HAVING Count(1) >1
```

```
SELECT txt, COUNT(*)
FROM dupes
GROUP BY txt HAVING COUNT(*) > 1;
```

```
SELECT id, COUNT( id ) AS cnt,
FROM myTable
GROUP BY id HAVING cnt > 1
```

Remove duplicate entries.

Assume the following table and data.

```
CREATE TABLE IF NOT EXISTS dupTest
(pkey int(11) NOT NULL auto_increment,
a int, b int, c int, timeEnter timestamp(14),
PRIMARY KEY  (pkey));
```

```
insert into dupTest (a,b,c) values (1,2,3),(1,2,3),
(1,5,4),(1,6,4);
```

Note, the first two rows contains duplicates in columns a and b. It contains other duplicates; but, leaves the other duplicates alone.

```
ALTER IGNORE TABLE  dupTest ADD UNIQUE INDEX(a,b);
```

Functions

(Mysql 5.0+)

There are also a number of functions available within MySQL that you may have used before, such as GREATEST() or CONCAT(). You can create your own **User Defined Functions**

```
DROP FUNCTION IF EXISTS helloworld;

CREATE FUNCTION helloworld() RETURNS VARCHAR(20)
BEGIN
RETURN "hello world 2";
END
```

Procedures

(Mysql 5.0+)

Stored procedures are sections of code which are stored in the database and executable within the database.

They fall in to two categories, functions and procedures.

```
DROP PROCEDURE IF EXISTS helloprocedure;
//
CREATE PROCEDURE helloprocedure()
BEGIN
SELECT 'hello procedure 2' ;
END
//
CALL helloprocedure();
```

Procedures can do a little more than functions, they do not need to return anything but can if needed return many things.

Procedures cannot be run from within SQL statements like functions, but must be called.

appendix 1 - Select examples

```sql
SELECT FORMAT(12332.123456, 4)

SELECT payee, SUM(amount)
FROM checks
GROUP BY payee

SELECT buyerid, MAX(price)
FROM antiques
GROUP BY buyerid

SELECT buyerid
FROM antiques
WHERE price > (SELECT AVG(price) + 100 FROM antiques)

SELECT buyerid FROM antiques
UNION
SELECT ownerid FROM orders

SELECT SUBSTRING_INDEX(surname,' ',-1) AS r
FROM advisers
ORDER BY r

SELECT ListName, COUNT(*), SUM(Info IS NOT NULL)
FROM ListTable
GROUP BY ListName
```

```sql
SELECT lname, teamno, game_pts, sport_pts, ref_pts,
adjust_ref_pts,
CASE
WHEN ref_pts + adjust_ref_pts > 15 THEN game_pts + 15
ELSE game_pts + ref_pts + adjust_ref_pts
END
AS total_pts,
CASE
WHEN ref_pts + adjust_ref_pts > 15 THEN 15 ELSE ref_pts +
adjust_ref_pts
END
AS total_ref_pts
FROM points
WHERE division = 'U14B'
ORDER BY total_pts DESC

SELECT IF(COUNT(*),"Available","Not Available")
As ProductStatus
FROM tb_Product
WHERE ProductName = "MyProduct"

SELECT studentid, AVG(number_grade) AS average_grade,
SUM(IF(letter_grade = 'A', 1, 0)) AS A_count,
SUM(IF(letter_grade = 'B+', 1, 0)) AS B+_count,
SUM(IF(letter_grade = 'B', 1, 0)) AS B_count,
SUM(IF(letter_grade = 'B-', 1, 0)) AS B-_count,
SUM(IF(letter_grade = 'C', 1, 0)) AS C_count,
FROM grades_table
GROUP BY studentid
```

```
SELECT ident, job_coop, cycle, lpad(status,10,' ') as status, type,
file_size, date_format(queue_time,'%Y-%m-%d %T') as
queue_time, file_time, rransfer_start, transfer_end
FROM queue
WHERE queue_time >= @Start AND queue_time < @End
ORDER BY ident

SELECT PartNumber, Qty
FROM product
ORDER BY Qty DESC LIMIT 122, 1;

SELECT COUNT(IF(inventory>0,NULL,1))
FROM product

SELECT COUNT(DISTINCT IF(balance>0,field,NULL))
FROM product

SELECT IF(users.phone IS NULL, 'NOT ENTER', users.phone)
phonefield
FROM users;

SELECT ID, quote, author
FROM quotes
ORDER BY RAND() LIMIT 1

SELECT ip, count(*)
FROM iptable
GROUP BY ip
ORDER BY 2 DESC limit 10;
```

```sql
SELECT slot , SUM(IF(day=1,1,0)) AS day1 ,
SUM(IF(day=2,1,0)) AS day2, SUM(IF(day=3,1,0))
AS day3, SUM(IF(day=4,1,0)) AS day4,
SUM(IF(day=5,1,0)) AS day5
FROM schedule
GROUP BY slot

SELECT e.e_id , e.e_code , COUNT(DISTINCT
qxe.q_id) AS e_count,
AVG(ratings.r_quality) AS avqual
FROM e, qxe, ratings
WHERE e.e_id = qxe.e_id AND ratings.e_id = e.e_id
AND ratings.q_id = qxe.q_id
GROUP BY e.e_id, e.e_code

SELECT symbol,
((SUM(buyrate*quantity))/SUM(quantity)) AS average
FROM portfolio
GROUP BY symbol;

SELECT c.id , c.campaign_name , COUNT(1) AS total,
SUM(IF(a.status='optin',1,0)) AS optin,
SUM(IF(a.status='optout',1,0)) AS optout
FROM addresses AS a

SELECT id
FROM stats
WHERE salary BETWEEN 30000 AND 50000
```

```
SELECT id
FROM stats
WHERE salary NOT BETWEEN 30000 AND 50000
```

appendix 2 - Join examples

```
SELECT t1.id FROM t1
LEFT JOIN t2 ON t1.id = t2.id
LEFT JOIN t3 ON t1.id = t3.id
WHERE t2.id IS NULL AND t3.id IS NULL;

SELECT p.name AS parent, c.name AS child,
MIN((TO_DAYS(NOW())-TO_DAYS(c.dob))/365) AS minage
FROM people AS p
LEFT JOIN people AS c
ON p.name=c.parent WHERE c.name IS NOT NULL
GROUP BY parent HAVING minage > 50
ORDER BY p.dob;

SELECT parent.id, parent.name,
SUM(IF(child.parent_id IS NULL, 0, 1)) AS CountChildren
FROM parent
LEFT JOIN child
ON parent.id=child.parent_id GROUP BY parent.id;

SELECT trucks.id, SUM(history.time_sec) AS total_seconds
FROM trucks
```

```sql
LEFT JOIN history ON trucks.id = history_truckid
GROUP BY trucks.id
ORDER BY total_seconds DESC

SELECT Events.ID, Events.ownerID,
Owners.ownerID
FROM Events
LEFT JOIN Events AS Owners
ON Events.ownerID=Owners.ownerID AND
Events.eventData> 3 MONTHS AGO
WHERE Owners.ownerID IS NULL

SELECT if (u.user_passwd <> nu.user_passwd, '*',"")
as CONFLICT, nu.*, u.*
FROM new_user_info nu INNER JOIN user_info u
ON nu.login_name = u.login_name

SELECT users.user_id
FROM users
LEFT JOIN comps_users_link ON
(users.user_id=comps_users_link.user_id)
WHERE comps_users_link.computer_id IS NULL

SELECT COUNT(B.Booking_ID), U.User_Location
FROM Users U
LEFT OUTER JOIN Bookings B ON U.User_ID = B.Rep_ID AND
B.Project_ID = '10'
GROUP BY(U.User_Location)
```

```sql
SELECT portfolio.symbol
FROM portfolio LEFT JOIN scripts
on portfolio.symbol = scripts.symbol
WHERE scripts.symbol IS NULL

SELECT continents.*, nations.*
FROM nations LEFT JOIN continents
ON (nations.CCode=continents.CCode)

SELECT global_lead.id, rep_no, es.fname as sales_name,
em.fname as marketing_name
FROM global_lead
LEFT JOIN global_employee es ON
global_lead.rep_no = es.id
LEFT JOIN global_employee em
ON global_lead.entered_by = em.id
WHERE global_lead.rep_no = 8

SELECT resume.Section_Value, candidate.Location
FROM resume
INNER JOIN candidate
ON candidate.id = resume.candidate_id
WHERE resume.Section_ID = '1' AND MATCH
(resume.Section_Value) AGAINST ('html') AND
candidate.Location LIKE '%CA%' OR 'California'
```

```sql
SELECT i.IDItems, i.Name, IFNULL(inv.Qty, 0) AS Qty
FROM Items i LEFT JOIN Invoice inv
ON i.IDItems = inv.IDItems
AND inv.IDInvoice = 1001

SELECT a.ID, a.First, a.Last, a.Email
FROM producta_customers a INNER JOIN
productb_customers b
ON a.email=b.email

SELECT a.*
FROM ProductsOLD a LEFT JOIN ProductsNEW b
ON a.Vendor = b.Vendor AND a.ID = b.ID
WHERE b.ID IS NULL
```

appendix 3 - Subselect

Delete employees in sales offices in Mumbai MU with
quotas over 40,000 Hint: Remember you have to
delete FROM a single table. Use a subquery.

```sql
DELETE * FROM SalesReps
WHERE RepNbr IN (SELECT RepNbr FROM
SalesReps, Offices
WHERE OfficeNbr = RepOffice AND
Quota>40000 AND State="MU");
```

```sql
select name, avg(amount) from salesreps, orders
where empl_num = rep and mfr = 'ACI'
group by name
having avg(amount) > (select avg(amount) from orders);
```

```sql
SELECT buyerid
FROM antiques
WHEi·E price > (SELECT AVG(price) + 100 FROM antiques);
```

```sql
SELECT ownerlastname
FROM owner
WHERE ownerid IN (SELECT DISTINCT buyerid FROM
antiques);
```

appendix 4 - create table

```sql
CREATE TABLE articles (
id INT UNSIGNED AUTO_INCREMENT NOT NULL
PRIMARY KEY,
title VARCHAR(200),
body TEXT,
FULLTEXT (title,body));
```

```sql
CREATE TABLE newBooks SELECT books.*,
publisher.id AS publisherId
FROM books, publisher
WHERE books.publisher = publisher.publisher
```

```
CREATE TABLE newtable SELECT DISTINCT *
FROM oldtable

CREATE TABLE t_merge (id INT NOT NULL, c
CHAR(10) NOT NULL,
KEY(id)) TYPE=MERGE UNION=(t1, t2);

CREATE TEMPORARY TABLE tmp SELECT
sub_id, MAX(date) AS date
FROM test3
GROUP BY sub_id;

CREATE TEMPORARY TABLE support_cost
(PRIMARY KEY serial) SELECT serial, SUM(cost)
FROM conveyor, support
WHERE conveyor.serial = support.serial GROUP BY serial;
```

Statement to load data:
```
LOAD DATA INFILE '/tmp/sp500hst.txt' INTO TABLE stocks
FIELDS TERMINATED BY ','
(date,ticker,open,high,low,close,volume);
```

appendix 5 - Merge table example

```
drop table if exists 'hindi';
CREATE TABLE 'hindi' (
    'tag' int(99) default NULL,
    'name' varchar(99) default NULL
) TYPE=MyISAM;
```

```
insert into hindi (tag, name) values (2, 'do');
insert into hindi values (3, 'teen');
insert into hindi values (4, 'char'), (5, 'paanch');

drop table if exists 'english';
CREATE TABLE 'english' (
    'tag' int(99) default NULL,
    'name' varchar(99) default NULL
) TYPE=MyISAM;
insert into english (tag, name) values (1, 'one');
insert into english values (2, 'two'), (3, 'three');

CREATE TABLE 'learn' (
    'tag' int(99) default NULL,
    'name' varchar(99) default NULL
) TYPE=MRG_MyISAM UNION=(hindi,english)
```

Notes

Notes

Notes

Notes

Computers

Shroff Original Titles
Launching The X Team Series
(An Imprint of Shroff Publishers)

PUBLISHED TITLE

ISBN	Title	Author	Price
8173666849	Application Development with Oracle & PHP on Linux for Beginners (B / CD-ROM), *828 Pages*	Bayross	550.00

FORTHCOMING TITLES

ISBN	Title	Author	Price
8173670048	Eclipse 3.1 for Beginners, *600 Pages*	Bayross	TBA
8173670056	J2EE 5 Server Programming for Professionals, *1,400 Pages*	Bayross	TBA
8173670064	Linux Programming for Beginners, *800 Pages*	Bayross	TBA
8173670153	MySQL 5 for Beginners, *600 Pages*	Bayross	TBA
8173670188	Oracle 10g for Beginners, *1,000 Pages*	Bayross	TBA
8173670218	Oracle 10g for Professionals, *1,200 Pages*	Bayross	TBA
8173670242	PHP 5.1 for Beginners, *600 Pages*	Bayross	TBA
8173670404	PHP 5.1 for Professionals, *800 Pages*	Bayross	TBA

Coming Soon under The X Team Series

Microsoft Platform

ISBN	Title	Author	Price
8173670773	.NET 2.0 Framework for Professionals, *000 Pages*	TBA	TBA
8173670781	.NET 2.0 Remoting for Professionals, *000 Pages*	TBA	TBA
8173670498	ASP .NET 2.0 with VB 2005 & Visual C# 2005 for Beginners, *000 Pgs*	TBA	TBA
8173670501	ASP .NET 2.0 with VB 2005 & Visual C# 2005 for Professionals, *000 Pages*	TBA	TBA
817367079X	SQL Server 2005 for Beginners, *000 Pages*	TBA	TBA
8173670803	SQL Server 2005 for Professionals, *000 Pages*	TBA	TBA
8173670811	SQL Server 2005 Reporting Services for Professionals, *000 Pages*	TBA	TBA
8173670757	Visual C# 2005 for Beginners, *000 Pages*	TBA	TBA
8173670765	Visual C# 2005 for Professionals, *000 Pages*	TBA	TBA
8173670730	Visual Basic 2005 for Beginners, *000 Pages*	TBA	TBA
8173670749	Visual Basic 2005 for Professionals, *000 Pages*	TBA	TBA
817367082X	Visual Studio 2005 Team Systems for Professionals, *000 Pages*	TBA	TBA

Java Platform

ISBN	Title	Author	Price
8173670838	EJB 3 for Professionals, *000 Pages*	TBA	TBA
8173670846	J2EE 5 for Beginners, *000 Pages*	TBA	TBA

ISBN	Title	Author	Price
8173670854	JSP 3 for Programmers, *000 Pages*	TBA	TBA
8173670862	Spring 1.2 for Beginners, *000 Pages*	TBA	TBA
Open Sources			
8173670870	Apache Tomcat 5.5 for Professionals, *000 Pages*	TBA	TBA
8173670889	XML for Professionals, *000 Pages*	TBA	TBA

Other Titles

ISBN	Title	Author	Price
8173669600	The Art of Creative Destruction: Illustrated Software Testing & Test Automation, *280 Pages*	Puranik	250.00
8173669988	Database Concepts and Systems, 2/ed, *292 Pages*	Bayross	275.00
8173667942	Operating System Concepts and Principles, *346 Pages*	George	275.00
8173668019	Software Defect Prevention Concepts and Implementation, *180 Pages (Hardbound)*	Kane & Bajaj	300.00
8173668817	Strategic Bidding: A Successful Approach (for IT / Consultancy), *192 Pages*	Garg	250.00

FORTHCOMING TITLES

ISBN	Title	Author	Price
8173665806	First Encounter with Java Including BlueJ, *000 Pages*	Shefali Bhutta	TBA
8173670897	Database Managment Systems - Core Concept, *000 Pages*	Ghosh	TBA

Shroff / Apress
(Apress Original Titles in Indian Reprints)

PUBLISHED TITLES

ISBN	Title	Author	Price
8181281101	.NET Game Programming with DirectX 9.0, VB .NET Edition **(B / CD-ROM)**, *654 Pages*	Lobao	550.00
8181280563	.NET System Management Service, *442 Pages*	Golomshok	400.00
8181280539	Advanced .NET Remoting, C# Edition, *424 Pages*	Rammer	375.00
8181280555	Applied ADO .NET: Building Data Driven Solutions, *956 Pages*	Chand	675.00
8181281063	ASP .NET 2.0 Revealed, *408 Pages*	Lorenz	375.00
8181280547	ATL Server: High Performance C++ on .NET, *520 Pages*	Kumar	450.00
8181280903	Automating Unix and Linux Administration, *600 Pages*	Bauer	500.00
8181281713	Beginning ASP .NET 1.1 in VB .NET from Novice to Professional, *1,008 Pages*	MacDonald	675.00
8181280989	C # Programmer's Handbook, *528 Pages*	Pearce	500.00
8181281314	Code Generation in Microsoft .NET, *760 Pages*	Dollard	525.00
8181280598	Comprehensive VB .NET Debugging, *528 Pages*	Pearce	450.00
1590590937	Database Programming with C#, *696 Pages*	Thomsen	400.00
8181280784	Debugging Strategies for .NET Developers, *272 Pages*	Dillon	250.00
818128108X	Designing Scalable .NET Applications, *568 Pages*	Rossberg	475.00
8181280741	Developing .NET Enterprise Applications, *528 Pages*	Kanalakis	425.00
8181280660	Enterprise Java for SAP, *336 Pages*	Sincock	325.00

ISBN	Title	Author	Price
8181281705	Essential PHP Tools: Modules, Extensions, and Accelerators, 368 Pages	Sklar	350.00
8181281055	Introduction to 3D Game Engine Design Using DirectX 9 and C#, 424 Pages	Harrison	375.00
8181281667	Ivor Horton's Beginning ANSI C++: The Complete Language, 3/ed, 1,118 Pages	Horton	750.00
8181281675	Java Regular Expressions, 276 Pages	Habibi	325.00
8181281098	JBoss 3.2 Deployment and Administration, 368 Pages	Kunnumpurath	325.00
8181280768	Learn VB .NET Through Game Programming, 400 Pages	Tagliaferri	350.00
8181280806	Managed C++ and .NET Development, 976 Pages	Fraser	675.00
818128120	Mastering Oracle PL/SQL Pracatical Solutions (Preview 10g), 648 Pages	McDonald	475.00
8181281047	Maximizing .NET Performance, 304 Pages	Wienholt	275.00
8181281209	Maximizing Performance Scalability with IBM WebSphere (covers Version 4 & 5), 576 Pages	Neat	500.00
8181281322	Oracle JDeveloper 10g Empowering J2EE Development, 294 Pages	Oak	325.00
8181280687	Peer - to - Peer with VB .NET, 440 Pages	MacDonald	400.00
8181280776	Performance Tuning and Optimizing ASP .NET Applications, 392 Pages	Hasan	375.00
8181280946	Practical Python, 648 Pages	Hetland	525.00
8181281071	Pro JSP, 3/ed (covers 2.0 and Servlet 2.4), 624 Pages	Brown	350.00
8181280954	The Qmail Handbook, 512 Pages	Sill	425.00
8181280792	Real World .NET Applications, 624 Pages	Kurniawan	500.00
8181280679	Real World ASP .NET Best Practices, 224 Pages	Muhammad	225.00
818128058X	Real World Enterprise Reports Using VB6 and VB .NET, 692 Pages	Ganz, Jr	550.00
8181280210	Software Exorcism: A Handbook for Debugging and Optimizing Legacy Code, 376 Pages	Blunden	325.00
1590590759	The Sun Certified Java Developer Exam with J2SE 1.4, 384 Pages	Habibi	300.00
8181280571	Web Services Patterns: Java Edition, 356 Pages	Monday	325.00
8181280601	WebSphere Studio Application Developers 5.0: Practical J2EE Development, 656 Pages	Livshin	525.00

Shroff / Apress

(Formerly under Wrox Press)

TITLES AT REDUCED PRICES

ISBN	Title	Author	Price
8173661448	ADO 2.6 Programmer's Reference, 720 Pages	Sussman	200.00
8173661464	ASP 3.0 Programmers Reference, 1,344 Pages	Anderson	250.00
8173661502	Beginning ASP Databases, 868 Pages	Kauffan	250.00
8173661529	Beginning Components for ASP, 868 Pages	Anderson	250.00

ISBN	Title	Author	Price
817366143X	Beginning E-Commerce with VB, ASP, SQL Server 7.0 & MTS, 802 Pages	Reynolds	250.00
8173661545	Beginning Java 2 - JDK 1.3 Edition, 1,272 Pages	Horton	375.00
817366160X	Beginning Java Object: From Concepts to Code, 696 Pages	Barker	200.00
8173661642	Beginning XHTML, 768 Pages	Boumphrey	250.00
8173663238	Data-Centric .NET Programing with C#, 812 Pages	Ferracchiati	325.00
8173661707	Enterprise Application Architecture with VB, ASP, MTS, 816 Pages	Moniz	325.00
8173661685	Java Programmer's Reference, 1.252 Pages	Palmer	325.00
8173661855	JavaScript Programmer's Reference (B / CD-ROM), 1,004 Pages	Wootton	275.00
817366157X	Professional Application Centre 2000, 432 Pages	Homer	175.00
8173661634	Professional ASP Data Access, 1,340 Pages	Esposito	350.00
8173662959	Professional ASP XML, 920 Pages	Baartse	250.00
8173662444	Professional BizTalk, 732 Pages	Mohr	200.00
8173662967	Professional ColdFusion 5, 1,240 Pages	Ambrose-Haynes	350.00
8173663505	Professional Commerce Server 2000 Programming, 1,126 Pages	Wrox	350.00
8173661898	Professional DCOM Application Development, 496 Pages	Pinnock	150.00
8173661901	Professional DCOM Programming, 592 Pages	Grimes	150.00
8173662452	Professional J2EE Programming with BEA Web Logic Server, 538 Pages	Gomez	100.00
8173661863	Professional Java Programming, 1,144 Pages	Spell	275.00
8173662029	Professional Site Server 3.0 Commerce Edition, 736 Pages	Tabini	250.00
8173663084	Professional Windows DNA: Building Distributed Web Applications with Visual Basic, COM+, MSMQ, SOAP & ASP, 1,016 Pages	Blexrud	350.00
PUBLISHED TITLES			
8173664692	.NET Compact Framework, 188 Pages	Morris	150.00
8173661456	.NET Enterprise Development in C#: From Design to Deployment, 474 Pages	Reynolds	325.00
8173661553	.NET Enterprise Development in VB .NET: From Design to Deployment, 470 Pages	Reynolds	350.00
8173666342	A C# Application from Inspiration to Implementation, 382 Pages	Dunn	350.00
8173666946	Apache Tomcat Security Handbook, 244 Pages	Chopra	250.00
8173666407	ASP To ASP .NET Migration Handbook, 312 Pages	Conway	275.00
8173664862	ASP .NET 1.0 with C#: Namespace Reference, 966 Pages	Kalani	650.00
8173664870	ASP .NET 1.0 with VB .NET: Namespace Reference, 924 Pages	Kalani	650.00
8173662355	ASP .NET Distributed Data Applications, 680 Pages	Homer	500.00
8173666415	ASP .NET E-Commerce Programming; Problem – Design - Solution: C# Edition, 372 Pages	Hoffman	350.00
8173662436	Axis: The Next Generation of Java SOAP, 294 Pages	Irani	225.00
8173666318	BEA WebLogic Server 7.0 Handbook: Deployment and Administration, 456 Pages	Mulder	375.00

ISBN	Title	Author	Price
8173666466	Beginning .NET Web Services using C#, 368 Pages	Bustos	325.00
8173664951	Beginning .NET Web Services using VB .NET, 360 Pages	Bustos	300.00
8173664889	Beginning ASP .NET 1.0 Databases using C#, 476 Pages	Kauffman	350.00
8173661510	Beginning ATL 3 COM Programming, 548 Pages	Grimes	450.00
8173664897	Beginning C# Databases, 664 Pages	Allen	500.00
8173666350	Beginning C# Web Applications with Visual Studio .NET, 628 Pages	Cazzulino	550.00
8173662827	Beginning Databases with MySQL, 600 Pages	Matthew	500.00
8173664137	Beginning Databases with PostgreSQL, 592 Pages	Stones	475.00
8173666970	Beginning J2EE 1.4, 740 Pages	Mukhar	475.00
8173663998	Beginning Java Networking, 832 Pages	Darby	550.00
8173666458	Beginning Java Web Services, 500 Pages	Bequet	400.00
8173666385	Beginning JSP 2.0: Build Web Applications Using JSP, Java, and Struts, 866 Pages	Galbraith	500.00
8173662738	Beginning Oracle Programming, 1,132 Pages	Dillon	675.00
8173661774	Beginning Perl, 704 Pages	Cozens	500.00
8173661669	Beginning SQL Programming (B / CD-ROM), 752 Pages	Kauffman	575.00
8173663181	Beginning SQL Server 2000 for Visual Basic Developers, 888 Pages	Willis	600.00
8173663467	Beginning SQL Server 2000 Programming (B / CD-ROM), 796 Pages	Dewson	600.00
817366420X	Beginning VB .NET Databases, 716 Pages	Forgey	350.00
8173660417	Beginning Visual Basic 6,920 Pages	Wright's	500.00
8173661626	Beginning Visual Basic 6 Database Programming, 888 Pages	Connell	600.00
8173662088	Beginning WAP, WML & WMLScript, 676 Pages	Lee	425.00
8173665958	Beginning Web Programming using VB.NET & Visual Studio .NET, 472 Pages	Bowes	400.00
817366644X	Building an ASP .NET Intranet, 484 Pages	Ardestani	425.00
8173666180	C# Class Design Handbook, 388 Pages	Conway	350.00
8173666121	C# Data Security Handbook, 300 Pages	MacDonald	325.00
8173661383	C# Programmer's Reference, 582 Pages	Palmer	475.00
8173666199	C# Threading Handbook, 296 Pages	Titus	275.00
8173663041	C# Web Services: Building Web Services with .NET Remoting and ASP .NET, 628 Pages	Banerjee	450.00
8173666296	Dissecting a C# Application: Inside SharpDevelop, 544 Pages	Holm	475.00
8173664080	Early Adopter HailStorm (.NET My Services), 244 Pages	Maharry	175.00
8173664048	Early Adopter J2SE 1.4, 218 Pages	Hart	175.00
817366238X	Early Adopter JSP Standard Tag Library, 322 Pages	Falkner	250.00
8173662940	Early Adopter JXTA: Peer-to-Peer Computing with Java, 312 Pages	Li	225.00

ISBN	Title	Author	Price
8173664005	Early Adopter VoiceXML, *328 Pages*	Andersson	250.00
8173662304	Early Adopter XQuery, *256 Pages*	Cagle	225.00
8173664714	Effective Visual Studio .NET, *600 Pages*	DeLoveh	450.00
8173666016	Expert One-on-One Advanced .NET Programming, *500 Pages*	Robinson	450.00
8173663874	Expert One-on-One Oracle, *1,328 Pages*	Kyte	850.00
8173667020	Expert One-on-One Visual Basic .NET Business Objects, *714 Pages*	Lhotka	600.00
817366496X	Fast Track ADO .NET: C# Edition, *322 Pages*	Ardestani	300.00
8173661928	Fast Track ASP .NET: C# Edition, *356 Pages*	Bellinaso	250.00
8173663033	Fast Track C#, *450 Pages*	Allen	350.00
8173664730	Fast Track VB .NET, *502 Pages*	Hollis	375.00
8173666393	IBM WebSphere 4.0 Application Server Deployment & Administration Handbook, *450 Pages*	Sharman	400.00
817366174X	Implementing LDAP, *518 Pages*	Wilcox	375.00
8173661758	Instant UML, *368 Pages*	Muller	300.00
8173664803	J2EE Design Patterns Applied, *450 Pages*	Berry	300.00
817366322X	Oracle 9i Java Programming: Solutions for Developers Using PL/SQL and Java, *884 Pages*	Holm	575.00
8173666504	PHP MySQL Website Programming: Problem–Design–Solution, *630 Pages*	Lea	500.00
8173666148	Professional .NET for Java Developers with C#, *448 Pages*	Lunn	350.00
8173664013	Professional .NET Framework, *760 Pages*	Hoffman	600.00
8173666369	Professional .NET Network Programming, *508 Pages*	Krowczyk	450.00
8173661790	Professional Active Server Pages 3.0, *1,316 Pages*	Homer	750.00
8173664056	Professional ADO .NET Programming, *746 Pages*	Joshi	600.00
817366613X	Professional ADO .NET with VB .NET, *614 Pages*	Dickinson	525.00
8173664757	Professional Apache 2.0, *902 Pages*	Wainwright	675.00
8173666482	Professional Apache Security, *386 Pages*	Mobily	375.00
8173661154	Professional ASP .NET Security, *472 Pages*	Basiura	375.00
817366451X	Professional ASP .NET Server Controls, *462 Pages*	Butler	350.00
8173664242	Professional ASP .NET Web Services, *792 Pages*	Basiura	600.00
8173664986	Professional ASP .NET Web Services with VB .NET, *808 Pages*	Basiura	550.00
8173666997	Professional C# Design Patterns Applied, *374 Pages*	Fischer	350.00
8173665567	Professional Design Patterns in VB .NET - Building Adaptable Application, *366 Pages*	Fischer	300.00
8173664064	Professional ebXML Foundations, *724 Pages*	Chappell	550.00
8173663513	Professional EJB, *1,200 Pages*	Adatia	750.00
8173663157	Professional J2EE EAI, *958 Pages*	Juric	600.00
8173661022	Professional Java E-Commerce, *1,034 Pages*	Allamaraju	400.00

ISBN	Title	Author	Price
8173662932	Professional Java Security, 544 Pages	Garms	350.00
8173660212	Professional Java Server Programming 3/ed - 1.3 J2EE Edition Version, 1,284 Pages	Allamaraju	675.00
817366255X	Professional Java Servlets 2.3, 740 Pages	Bell	600.00
8173662908	Professional Java SOAP, 546 Pages	Bequet	350.00
8173662614	Professional Java Web Services, 514 Pages	Hendricks	450.00
8173661804	Professional Java XML, 1,188 Pages	Ahmed	750.00
8173664536	Professional JavaScript, 2/ed, 1,192 Pages	Baartse	850.00
8173662975	Professional Jini, 928 Pages	Li	575.00
817366172?	Professional JMS Programming, 800 Pages	Giotta	350.00
817366246G	Professional JSP Tag Libraries, 492 Pages	Brown	350.00
8173661820	Professional JSP, 2/ed, 1,228 Pages	Brown	750.00
8173661960	Professional Linux Deployment, 1,000 Pages	Prasad	500.00
8173662002	Professional Linux Programming, 1,196 Pages	Matthew	850.00
8173661979	Professional MFC with Visual C++ 6, 1,248 Pages	Blaszczak	850.00
8173331812	Professional Oracle8i Application Prog with Java, PL/SQL & XML, 1,248 Pages	Carnell	575.00
8173663696	Professional Perl Development, 750 Pages	Kobes	450.00
817366305X	Professional Perl Programming, 1,248 Pages	Wainwright	850.00
817366630X	Professional PHP Web Services, 502 Pages	Fuller	500.00
8173666008	Professional SCWCD Certification (B / CD-ROM), 480 Pages	Dalton	400.00
8173664099	Professional SQL Server 2000 Data Warehousing with Analysis Services, 708 Pages	Bain	450.00
8173663572	Professional SQL Server 2000 Database Design, 628 Pages	Davidson	575.00
8173663556	Professional SQL Server 2000 XML, 622 Pages	Burke	400.00
8173666210	Professional Visual Basic 6: A 2003 Programmer's Resource (B / CD-ROM), 674 Pages	Ablan	600.00
8173662134	Professional VB .NET Transactions, 552 Pages	Bortniker	350.00
8173661839	Professional Visual Basic Interoperability - COM & VB6 to .NET, 446 Pages	Hollis	325.00
817366210X	Professional WAP, 832 Pages	Wrox	600.00
8173666091	Professional Web Services Security, 630 Pages	Galbraith	550.00
8173663351	Professional Windows Forms, 708 Pages	Bell	500.00
8173662037	Professional XML 2/ed, 1,000 Pages	Birbeck	675.00
8173663122	Professional XML for .NET Developers, 754 Pages	Dalvi	550.00
8173663076	Professional XSL, 800 Pages	Cagle	500.00
8173666490	SQL Server 2000 Stored Procedures Handbook, 292 Pages	Bain	250.00
8173665370	Understanding the .NET Framework, 280 Pages	Tegels	225.00

ISBN	Title	Author	Price
817366482X	VB .NET & SQL Server 2000 - Building an Effective Data Layer, 582 Pages	Bain	475.00
8173661693	Visual Basic .NET Class Design Handbook, 396 Pages	Olsen	325.00
8173665028	Visual Basic .NET Code Security Handbook, 312 Pages	Lippert	225.00
8173666431	Visual Basic .NET Debugging Handbook, 332 Pages	Narkiewicz	300.00
8173665036	Visual Basic .NET Deployment Handbook, 320 Pages	Delorme	250.00
8173666059	Visual Basic .NET Reflection Handbook, 264 Pages	Hart	225.00
8173664943	Visual Basic .NET Remoting Handbook, 278 Pages	Curran	225.00
8173666075	Visual Basic .NET Serialization Handbook, 338 Pages	Olsen	300.00
8173665583	Visual Basic .NET Solutions Toolkit: 30 Pratical Components for .NET, 466 Pages	Lhotka	375.00
8173664838	Visual Basic .NET Text Manipulation Handbook, 294 Pages	Liger	225.00
8173664846	Visual Basic .NET Threading Handbook, 278 Pages	Ardestani	225.00
8173665974	Visual Basic .NET Windows Services Handbook, 218 Pages	Conway	225.00
8173665540	Visual C# .NET: A Guide for VB6 Developers, 556 Pages	Maiani	450.00
8173664765	Visual C++ .NET: A Primer for C++ Developers, 486 Pages	Corera	350.00
8173664706	Web Services Faceplates, 304 Pages	Mohr	225.00
8173662290	XML Applications, 600 Pages	Boumphrey	400.00
8173666474	XML Design Handbook, 332 Pages	Bonneau	350.00

Auerbach Publication

ISBN	Title	Author	Price
0849319978	Information Security Management Handbook, 5/ed, 2,088 Pgs.	Tipton	£ 68.00
0849320321	Information Technology Control & Audit, 2/ed, 888 Pages	Gallegos	£ 26.00
084931707X	Official (ISC)2 Guide to the CISSP Exam (B / CD-ROM), 930 Pages	Hansche	3,000.00
0849314798	Software Engineering Handbook, 896 Pages	Keyes	£ 63.00
0849325242	Software Testing and Continuous Quality Improvement (B / CD-ROM), 2/ed, 560 Pages	Lewis	£ 38.00

Shroff / Brainysoftware.com

ISBN	Title	Author	Price
8173664501	How Tomcat Works (Covers 4 & 5), 486 Pages	Kurniawan	375.00

Shroff / Charles River Media

ISBN	Title	Author	Price
8173660875	Applied Software Engineering Using Apache Jakarta Commons (B / CD-ROM), 436 Pages	Gross	400.00
8173660905	Code Hacking: A Developer's Guide to Network Security B / CD-ROM), 404 Pages	Conway	400.00
8173665346	Linux Network Security (B / CD-ROM), 564 Pages	Smith	475.00
8173660913	The Linux TCP/IP Stack: Networking for Embedded Systems (B / CD-ROM), 604 Pages	Herbert	450.00

ISBN	Title	Author	Price
8173669759	Software Testing Techniques: Finding the Defects that Matter, *388 Pages*	Loveland	350.00

FORTHCOMING TITLES

August 2005

ISBN	Title	Author	Price
8173661049	Creating Fractals (B / CD-ROM), *300 Pages*	Stevens	350.00
8173661472	Crystal Report 11 for Developer's (B / CD-ROM), *600 Pages*	McAmis	450.00
8173663963	Mathematics and Physics for Programmers (B / CD-ROM), *608 Pgs*	Kodicek	450.00
8173662533	Microprocessors: From Assembly Language to C Using the PIC18Fxx2 (B / CD-ROM), *450 Pages*	Reese	300.00
8173664579	The OpenGL Extensions Guide (B / CD-ROM), *670 Pages*	Lengyel	525.00

September 2005

ISBN	Title	Author	Price
8173670056	C++ Standard Library Practical Tips (B / CD-ROM), *300 Pages*	Reese	200.00
8173670102	Cryptographic Libraries for Developer's (B / CD-ROM), *400 Pages*	Kelly	400.00
8173670099	Java Messaging, *500 Pages*	Bruno	400.00
8173670072	Enterprise Web Services Security (B / CD-ROM), *400 Pages*	Hollar	400.00
8173670110	Programming Mobile Business Solutions Using Visual Studio 2005 (B / CD-ROM), *400 Pages*	Robbins	400.00
8173670080	SQL Server 2005 for Developer's (B / CD-ROM), *400 Pages*	Ericsson	400.00

CRC Press

ISBN	Title	Author	Price
0849308097	Software Testing: A Craftman's Approach, 2/ed, *384 Pages*	Jorgensen	£ 46.00
0849323665	Software Engineering Processess: Principles & Application, *752 Pages*	Wang	£ 60.00

Shroff / Curlingstone

(Curlingstone now an imprint of Apress)

ISBN	Title	Author	Price
8173666326	The Art and Science of Oracle Performance Tuning, *484 Pages*	Lawson	325.00
8173666989	Data Modeling for Everyone, *524 Pages*	Allen	400.00

Shroff / DVT Press

ISBN	Title	Author	Price
8173669171	The J2EE Architect's Handbook, *304 Pages*	Ashmore	300.00

Shroff / Endorf

ISBN	Title	Author	Price
8173667004	CISSP Study Guide 2/ed (2002-03 Updated ed), *568 Pages*	Endorf	300.00
8173667012	SSCP Study Guide Updated Edition, *292 Pages*	Endorf	225.00

Shroff / Friends of ED

(friends of ED now an imprint of Apress)

TITLES AT REDUCED PRICES

ISBN	Title	Author	Price
8173664196	Director 8.5 Studio (B / CD-ROM), *836 Pages*	Bauman	100.00
817366336X	Flash 5 Studio (B / CD-ROM), *798 Pages*	Adnani	100.00

ISBN	Title	Author	Price
8173663939	Flash & Director StudioLab, 516 Pages	Gould	75.00
8173663416	Flash XML StudioLab, 512 Pages	Tindale	75.00
8173663408	Foundation Director 8.5, 456 Pages	Utian	75.00
8173663386	Foundation Dreamweaver UltraDev, 480 Pages	Paddock	50.00
8173662126	Foundation Flash 5, 646 Pages	Bhangal	75.00
8173663459	Foundation Illustrator 10, 548 Pages	Loader	75.00
8173664552	Foundation Macromedia Flash MX, 704 Pages	Besley	75.00
8173664188	Foundation Photoshop 6 (Includes 8 Full Color Pages), 672 Pages	Smith	75.00
8173664595	Photoshop Elements Express, 250 Pages	Beckley	50.00
8173664609	Revolutionary After Effects 5.5 **(B / CD-ROM)**, 500 Pages	Kingsnorth	50.00

PUBLISHED TITLES

ISBN	Title	Author	Price
8181281594	Extending Macromedia Flash MX 2004: Complete Guide and Reference to JavaScript Flash, 472 Pages	Peters	425.00
8173662185	Foundation ActionScript, 512 Pages	Bhangal	300.00
8181281624	Foundation Macromedia Flash MX 2004, 488 Pages	Besley	425.00
1903450039	New Masters of Flash **(B / CD-ROM)**, 544 Pages [Size 9x10]	McIntyre	850.00
1903450365	New Masters of Flash: Annual 2002 **(B / CD-ROM)**, 544 Pages [Size 9x10]	McIntyre	850.00
1903450624	New Masters of Photoshop **(B / CD-ROM)**, 552 Pgs. [Size 9x10]	McIntyre	850.00

Shroff / John Wiley

ISBN	Title	Author	Price
0471469122	Art of Software Testing, 2/ed, 252 Pages	Meyers	$ 75.00
0471718890	**The Black Book of Outsourcing: How to Manage the Changes, Challenges, and Opportunites, 390 Pages**	**Brown**	**$ 29.95**
8173660387	Client/Server Programming with Java & Corba 2/ed **(B / CD-ROM)**, 1,072 Pages	Orfali	650.00
9971513714	Client/Server Survival Guide 3/ed, 795 Pages	Orfali	500.00
997151415X	The CISSP Prep Guide: Mastering the 10 Domain of Computer Security, 576 Pages	Krutz	200.00
997151415X	The Data Warehouse Lifecycle Toolkit **(B / CD-ROM)**, 792 Pages	Kimball	650.00
9814126144	The Data Warehouse Toolkit 2/ed, 460 Pages	Kimball	450.00
0471267686	Financial Modeling Using Excel & VBA **(B / CD-ROM)**, 672 Pages	Sengupta	$ 65.00
9971513579	Software Engineering: Principles & Practice 2/ed, 748 Pages	Van Vliet	500.00
9971514281	System Analysis & Design: An Object Oriented Approach with UML, 534 Pages	Dennis	450.00

Shroff / Labyrinth

ISBN	Title	Author	Price
8173665443	Computer Concepts & Windows, 130 Pages	Stolins	125.00
817366546X	Microsoft Excel 2002 - Level 1 **(B / DISK)**, 252 Pages	Favro	250.00

ISBN	Title	Author	Price
8173665478	Microsoft Office XP Comprehensive Course (B / DISK), 1,202 Pgs	Favro/Stolins	675.00
8173665451	Microsoft Word 2002 - Level 1 (B / DISK), 250 Pages	Favro/Stolins	250.00

Shroff / Manning

ISBN	Title	Author	Price
8173665389	J2EE & XML Development, 300 Pages	Gabrick	200.00
8173665397	JDK 1.4 Tutorial, 408 Pages	Travis	300.00
8173665400	Microsoft .NET for Programmers, 380 Pages	Grimes	275.00
8173665419	Web Development with Apache & Perl, 432 Pages	Petersen	300.00
8173665427	Web Development with JavaServer Pages, 2/ed, 804 Pages	Fields	450.00

Shroff / Many Worlds Productions

ISBN	Title	Author	Price
0970683081	Model, Rig, Animate! with 3ds max 6 (B / CD-ROM), 240 Pages	Bousquet	$ 35.00

Shroff / Mike Murach

ISBN	Title	Author	Price
8173669228	Murach's ASP .NET Web Programming with VB .NET, 736 Pages	Lowe	575.00
8173665532	**Murach's Beginning Java 2 JDK 5, 800 Pages**	**Doug**	**450.00**
8173669244	Murach's C#, 770 Pages	Murach	550.00
8173669236	Murach's JavaServlets & JSP: Training & Reference (B / CD-ROM), 642 Pages	Steelman	525.00
817366921X	Murach's VB .NET Database Programming with ADO. NET, 610 Pages	Prince	525.00

FORTHCOMING TITLES

ISBN	Title	Author	Price
8173668620	Murach's ASP.NET 2.0 Upgrader's Guide C# Edition, 546 Pages	Lowe	400.00
8173668698	Murach's ASP.NET 2.0 Upgrader's Guide VB Edition, 546 Pages	Lowe	400.00

US EDITIONS

ISBN	Title	Author	Price
1890774022	DB2 for the COBOL Programmer, Part 1 (2/ed), 431 Pages	Garvin	$ 45.00
1890774030	DB2 for the COBOL Programmer, Part 2 (2/ed), 402 Pages	Garvin	$ 45.00
0911625313	DOS/VSE Assembler Language, 492 Pages	McQuilen	$ 45.00
0911625364	DOS/VSE ICCF, 372 Pages	Eckols	$ 31.00
091162550X	DOS/VSE JCL, 2/ed, 445 Pages	Eckols	$ 45.00
0911625291	IMS for the COBOL Programmer, Part 1, 333 Pages	Eckols	$ 45.00
0911625305	IMS for the COBOL Programmer, Part 2, 398 Pages	Eckols	$ 45.00
1890774103	Murach's CICS Desk Reference, 592 Pages	Lowe	$ 49.50
189077409X	Murach's CICS for the COBOL Programmer, 633 Pages	Menendez	$ 54.00
1890774146	Murach's OS/390 and z/OS JCL, 559 Pages	Lowe	$ 62.50
1890774243	Murach's Mainframe COBOL, 687 Pages	Murach	$ 59.50
1890774057	Murach's Structured COBOL (B / CD-ROM), 800 Pages	Murach	$ 62.50
0911625569	MVS TSO, Part 1: Concepts and ISPF, 467 Pages	Lowe	$ 42.50
0911625577	MVS TSO, Part 2: Commands, CLIST, and REXX, 450 Pages	Lowe	$ 42.50
0911625348	MVS Assembler Language, 528 Pages	McQuillen	$ 45.00

ISBN	Title	Author	Price
0911625941	Structured COBOL Methods, *208 Pages*	Noll	$ 25.00
091162547X	VM / CMS: XEDIT Commands and Features, *225 Pages*	Eckols	$ 25.00
091162533X	VSAM: AMS and Application Programming, *260 Pages*	Lowe	$ 32.50
0911625463	VSAM for the COBOL Programmer, *187 Pages*	Lowe	$ 27.50

Shroff / No Starch Press

ISBN	Title	Author	Price
8173668078	The Art of Assembly Language (B / CD-ROM), *928 Pages*	Hyde	525.00
8173667365	The Book of Nero 6 Ultra Edition: CD and DVD Burning Made Easy, *216 Pages*	Ross	200.00
8173663130	**The Book of Postfix: State-of-the-Art Message Transport , *362 Pages***	Hildebrandt	425.00
8173667993	The Book of Wi-Fi, *288 Pages*	Ross	250.00
8173668566	The Book of VMWare, *268 Pages*	Ward	250.00
817366952X	Cisco Routers for the Desperate: Router Management, The Easy Way, *148 Pages*	Lucas	150.00
8173668388	Hacking: The Art of Exploitation, *256 Pages*	Erickson	225.00
8173668337	**How Linux Works, *392 Pages***	Ward	300.00
8173667977	How Not To Program in C++, *272 Pages*	Ouanline	175.00
8173668345	The Linux Cookbook, 2/ed, *826 Pages*	Stutz	600.00
8173668353	**The Linux Enterprise Cluster: Build a Highly Available Cluster with Commodity Hardware and Free Software (B / CD-ROM), *460 Pages***	Kopper	450.00
8173668825	Linux for Non-Geeks (B / CD-ROM), *336 Pages*	Grant	300.00
8173668876	The Official GNOME 2 Developer's Guide, *520 Pages*	Warkus	475.00
8173667985	Steal This Computer Book 3, *356 Pages*	Wang	350.00
8173669554	Stealing This File Sharing Book, *296 Pages*	Wang	300.00
8173668795	**Wicked Cool Shell Scripts, *368 Pages***	Taylor	350.00
8173668329	Write Great Code: Volume 1: Understanding the Machine, *464 Pgs*	Hyde	400.00
8173661871	**Writing Portable Code: A Guide to Developing Software for Multiple Platforms, *276 Pages***	Hook	275.00

FORTHCOMING TITLES

September 2005

ISBN	Title	Author	Price
8173670021	The Book of™ MaxDB: MySQL for the Enterprise (B / CD-ROM), *600 Pages*	Singleton	500.00
8173669392	Computer Security 101: What You Need to Know to Secure Your Computer or Network (B / CD-ROM), *250 Pages*	Bradley	250.00
8173670013	Linux Made Easy: The Official Guide to Xandros 3 for Everyday Users (B / CD-ROM), *496 Pages*	Grant	400.00
8173670129	Now Playing: Visual Basic 2005 Express (B / CD-ROM), *760 Pages*	Wang	500.00
8173664641	The TCP/IP Guide, *1,550 Pages*	Kozierok	850.00

ISBN	Title	Author	Price
8173670137	Wicked Cool Java: Code Bits, Open-Source Libraries and Project Ideas, 772 Pages	Eubanks	550.00
8173670048	Wicked Cool™ Perl Scripts Useful Perl Scripts That Solve Difficult Problems, 304 Pages	Oualline	300.00
8173670145	Write Great Code: Volume 2: Thinking Low - Level, Writing High - Level, 272 Pages	Hyde	275.00

Shroff / O'Reilly

TITLES AT REDUCED PRICES

ISBN	Title	Author	Price
8173663661	.NET Framework Essentials, 324 Pages	Thai	75.00
8173664277	Access Cookbook for 97, 2000 & 2002 (B / CD-ROM), 724 Pages	Getz	100.00
8173662231	ActionScript: The Definitive Guide, 726 Pages	Moock	150.00
8173662886	Building Oracle XML Applications (B / CD-ROM), 824 Pages	Muench	100.00
8173664250	Building Wireless Community Networks, 144 Pages	Flickenger	50.00
8173662584	Cascading Style Sheets: The Definitive Guide, 476 Pages	Meyer	75.00
8173662878	Developing ASP Components 2/ed, 864 Pages	Powers	100.00
817366272X	DHCP for Windows 2000, 288 Pages	Alcott	75.00
8173663599	Exim: The Mail Transport Agent, 638 Pages	Hazel	75.00
8173660573	Java Threads, 2/ed, 336 Pages	Oaks	75.00
8173664145	Java Cookbook, 890 Pages	Darwin	150.00
8173660557	Java Foundation Classes in a Nutshell, 752 Pages	Flanagan	75.00
8173662711	Java Internationalization, 456 Pages	Deitsch	75.00
8173663807	Java Programming with Oracle SQLJ, 404 Pages	Price	75.00
8173661103	JavaScript Application Cookbook, 512 Pages	Bradenbaugh	75.00
8173661111	JavaScript Pocket Reference, 96 Pages	Flanagan	25.00
8173662509	Jini in a Nutshell, 420 Pages	Oaks	75.00
8173662320	Learning Java (B / CD-ROM), 732 Pages	Niemeyer	75.00
8173660603	Learning Perl/Tk, 380 Pages	Walsh	75.00
8173661677	Learning Web Design: A Beginner's Guide to HTML, Graphics & Web Environment (2 Color Book), 432 Pages	Niederst	100.00
8173663173	Learning WML & WMLScript, 204 Pages	Frost	50.00
8173663149	Learning XML, 376 Pages	Ray	75.00
8173662193	MCSD in a Nutshell: The Visual Basic Exams, 636 Pages	Foxall	75.00
8173662398	MCSE in a Nutshell: The Windows 2000 Exams, 504 Pages	Moncur	75.00
8173662517	MP3: The Definitive Guide, 408 Pages	Hacker	75.00
8173660697	Oracle PL/SQL Language Pocket Reference, 80 Pages	Feuerstein	25.00
8173661243	Perl/Tk Pocket Reference, 104 Pages	Lidie	25.00
817366269X	PHP Pocket Reference, 124 Pages	Lerdorf	25.00
8173661251	PNG: The Definitive Guide, 344 Pages	Roelofs	50.00
817366126X	Practical Internet Groupware, 520 Pages	Udell	75.00

ISBN	Title	Author	Price
8173660751	Practical UNIX & Internet Security, 2/ed, 1,008 Pages	Garfinkel	150.00
8173660190	QuarkXPress in a Nutshell, 552 Pages	O'Quinn	50.00
8173662487	sed & awk Pocket Reference, 60 Pages	Robbins	25.00
8173661294	sendmail Desktop Reference, 74 Pages	Costales	25.00
8173662606	Tcl/Tk Pocket Reference, 100 Pages	Raines	25.00
8173663474	VB .NET Language in a Nutshell, 662 Pages	Roman	100.00
8173663475	Web Database Applications with PHP & MySQL, 600 Pages	Williams	75.00
8173661359	Webmaster in a Nutshell, 2/ed, 540 Pages	Spainhour	75.00
8173662630	Windows 2000 Active Directory, 624 Pages	Lowe-Norris	75.00
8173663327	Windows 2000 Performance Guide, 650 Pages	Friedman	75.00
8173663289	XML in a Nutshell, 400 Pages	Harold	100.00
8173662096	XSLT, 486 Pages	Tidwell	100.00
PUBLISHED TITLES			
8173666539	.NET and XML, 484 Pages	Bornstein	425.00
8173669201	.NET Compact Framework Pocket Guide, 122 Pages	Lee	125.00
8173666547	.NET Framework Essentials, 3/ed, 392 Pages	Thai	325.00
8173665729	**.NET Gotchas, 402 Pages**	**Subramaniam**	**300.00**
8173665753	802.11 Security, 200 Pages	Potter	175.00
8173664046	802.11 Wireless Networks: The Definitive Guide, 474 Pages	Gast	400.00
8173664285	Access Database Design & Programming, 3/ed, 454 Pages	Roman	325.00
8173666377	**Access Hacks: Tips & Tools for Wrangling**		
	Your Data, 362 Pgs	**Bluttman**	**325.00**
8173667233	ActionScript Cookbook, 904 Pages	Lott	675.00
8173666555	ActionScript for Flash MX Pocket Reference, 152 Pages	Moock	125.00
8173665761	ActionScript for Flash MX: The Definitive		
	Guide, 2/ed, 904 Pages	Colin Moock	750.00
8173666563	Active Directory for Windows Server 2003, 2/ed, 692 Pages	Allen	575.00
8173667357	Active Directory Cookbook for Windows Server 2003 and		
	Windows 2000, 632 Pages	Allen	525.00
817366725X	ADO .NET Cookbook, 636 Pages	Hamilton	500.00
8173665222	ADO .NET for Visual Basic .NET 2003 in a Nutshell: A Desktop		
	Quick Reference (B / CD-ROM), 626 Pages	Hamilton	500.00
0596006004	Adobe Encore DVD: In the Studio, 336 Pages	Dixon	1,225.00
0596007361	Adobe InDesign CS One-on-One (B / CD-ROM), 400 Pages	McClelland	1,375.00
0596006187	Adobe Photoshop CS One-on-One (B / CD-ROM), 488 Pages	McClelland	1,225.00
8173668302	**Advanced Perl Programming, 2/ed, 308 Pages**	**Cozens**	**325.00**
8173668205	AI for Game Developers, 400 Pages	Bourg	375.00
8173669384	**AspectJ Cookbook, 364 Pages**	**Miles**	**350.00**
8173667292	Amazon Hacks: 100 Industrial Strength Tips & Tricks, 312 Pages	Bausch	250.00
8173665524	Ant: The Definitive Guide, 296 Pages	Tilly	275.00

ISBN	Title	Author	Price
8173665133	Apache: The Definitive Guide (Covers Apache 2.0 & 1.3) 3/ed, 594 Pages	Laurie	500.00
8173667446	Apache Cookbook (Covers Apache 2.0 & 1.3), 264 Pages	Coar	250.00
8173662525	Apache Pocket Reference, 112 Pages	Ford	75.00
8173662274	**Apache Security, 428 Pages**	**Ristic**	**400.00**
8173666571	ASP .NET Cookbook (Cover ASP .NET 1.1), 846 Pages	Kittel	700.00
8173667306	ASP .NET in a Nutshell: A Desktop Quick Reference, 2/ed, 1,008 Pages	Duthie	600.00
8173667837	**The Art of Project Management, 512 Pages**	**Berkun**	**350.00**
8173662347	AutoCAD 2000 In a Nutshell: A Command Reference Guide, 592 Pages	Kent	325.00
8173663955	Beginning Perl for Bioinformatics, 390 Pages	Tisdall	300.00
8173668981	Better, Faster, Lighter Java, 270 Pages	Tate	250.00
817366658X	BGP, 292 Pages	van Beijnum	275.00
8173665125	BLAST, 372 Pages	Korf	325.00
817366899X	BSD Hacks:100 Industrial-Strength Tips & Tools, 458 Pages	Lavigne	375.00
8173666598	Building Embedded Linux Systems, 422 Pages	Yaghmour	350.00
8173661014	Building Internet Firewalls 2/ed, 904 Pages	Chapman	650.00
8173662282	Building Java Enterprise Applications: Vol. 1 - Architecture, 324 Pages	McLaughlin	225.00
8173661391	Building Linux Clusters **(B / CD-ROM)**, 360 Pages	Spector	350.00
8173665621	Building Secure Servers with Linux, 454 Pages	Bauer	375.00
8173664749	**Building the Perfect PC, 360 Pages**	**Thompson**	**350.00**
8173666601	**C Pocket Reference, 142 Pages**	**Prinz**	**100.00**
8173664439	C# & VB .NET Conversion Pocket Reference, 156 Pages	Mojica	75.00
8173665885	C# Cookbook, 876 Pages	Teilhet	600.00
8173664293	C# Essentials, 2/ed, 224 Pages	Albahari	175.00
8173665192	C# Language Pocket Reference, 132 Pages	Drayton	100.00
8173663726	C# in a Nutshell: A Desktop Quick Reference, 864 Pages	Drayton	600.00
8173666628	C++ in a Nutshell, (Cover ISO/IEC 14882 STD) 816 Pages	Lischner	500.00
8173667101	C++ Pocket Reference, 148 Pages	Loudon	100.00
0596001088	The Cathedral & The Bazaar: Musings On Linux and Open Source by an Accidental Revolutionary, Revised & Expanded, 256 Pages	Raymond	525.00
8173669066	Cascading Style Sheets: The Definitive Guide (Covers CSS2 & CSS 2.1), 2/ed, 538 Pages	Meyer	475.00
8173662266	CDO & MAPI Programming with Visual Basic, 388 Pages	Grundgeiger	175.00
8173664269	CGI Programming on the World Wide Web, 454 Pages	Gundavaram	300.00
817366045X	CGI Programming with Perl, 476 Pages	Gundavaram	325.00
8173668469	**Classic Shell Scripting, 568 Pages**	**Robbins**	**425.00**

ISBN	Title	Author	Price
8173667241	Cisco Cookbook, *918 Pages*	Dooley	700.00
8173663653	COM & .NET Component Services, *390 Pages*	Lowy	250.00
8173663645	COM+ Programming with Visual Basic, *372 Pages*	Mojica	225.00
8173660638	Creating Effective JavaHelp, *196 Pages*	Lewis	125.00
8173669163	CSS Cookbook (Cover CSS 2.1), *280 Pages*	Schmitt	275.00
8173667802	**Database In Depth: The Relational Model for Practitioners, *250 Pgs***	C.J.Date	225.00
8173662363	Database Nation: The Death of Privacy in the 21st Century, *336 Pages*	Garfinkel	235.00
8173662894	Database Programming with JDBC & Java 2/ed, *348 Pages*	Reese	150.00
8173665664	Designing Embedded Hardware, *324 Pages*	Catsoulis	250.00
8173663882	Designing Large Scale LANs, *408 Pages*	Dooley	275.00
8173662428	Developing Bio-informatics Computer Skills, *504 Pages*	Gibas	225.00
8173669473	**Developing Feeds with RSS and Atom, *280 Pages***	Hammersley	300.00
0596005474	Digital Photography: Expert Techniques (Covers Photoshop CS), *496 Pages*	Milburn	1,375.00
0596006667	Digital Photography Hacks: 100 Industrial - Strength Tips & Tools, *336 Pages*	Story	800.00
0596006276	Digital Photography Pocket Guide, 2/ed, *128 Pages*	Story	500.00
0596009461	**Digital Video Hacks: Tips & Tools for Shooting, Editing & Sharing, *426 Pages***	Paul	800.00
0596005237	Digital Video Pocket Guide, *474 Pages*	Story	500.00
8173662983	DNS & BIND (Covers BIND 9), 4/ed, *642 Pages*	Albitz	500.00
8173665672	DNS & BIND Cookbook, *248 Pages*	Liu	250.00
8173663785	DNS on Windows 2000, 2/ed, *376 Pages*	Larson	275.00
8173660506	DNS on Windows NT, *352 Pages*	Albitz	195.00
8173662991	Dreamweaver MX: The Missing Manual, *750 Pages*	McFarland	600.00
8173665281	Dynamic HTML: The Definitive Reference, 2/ed, *1,428 Pages*	Goodman	650.00
8173669015	Eclipse (Coverage of 3.0), *344 Pages*	Holzner	325.00
8173669309	Eclipse Cookbook (Cover 3.0), *372 Pages*	Holzner	350.00
8173663017	Effective awk Programming, 3/ed, *454 Pages*	Robbins	325.00
8173667268	Enterprise JavaBeans (Covers EJB 2.1 & EJB 2.0 Includes workbook for JBoss 4.0), 4/ed, *798 Pages*	Monson - Haefel	500.00
8173668167	Enterprise Service Architecture - O'Reilly SAP Series, *236 Pages*	Woods	225.00
8173669317	Essential ActionScript 2.0, *528 Pages*	Moock	400.00
8173666784	**Enterprise Service Bus, *284 Pages***	Chappell	300.00
8173669430	**Essential SharePoint, *338 Pages***	Webb	325.00
8173663580	Essential SNMP, *338 Pages*	Mauro	300.00
817366529X	Essential System Administration, 3/ed, *1,178 Pages*	Frisch	525.00
8173666644	Essential System Administration Pocket Reference, *152 Pages*	Frisch	125.00

ISBN	Title	Author	Price
8173660255	Essential Windows NT System Administration, *488 Pages*	Frisch	225.00
8173662495	Ethernet: The Definitive Guide, *528 Pages*	Spurgeon	300.00
8173662754	Excel 2000 In a Nutshell: A Power User's Quick Reference, *560 Pages*	Simon	300.00
8173669619	Excel 2003 Personal Trainer (B / CD-ROM), (2 Color book) *490 Pages*	CustomGuide	550.00
8173668299	Excel 2003 Programming: A Developer's Notebook, *330 Pages*	Webb	325.00
8173668035	Excel: The Missing Manual, *802 Pages*	MacDonald	550.00
8173669406	Excel Annoyances: How to Fix the Most Annoying Things about Your Favorite Spreadsheet , *266 Pages*	Frye	275.00
8173668612	Excel Hacks: 100 Industrial Strength Tips & Tools, *316 Pages*	David	275.00
8173665257	Exploring the JDS Linux Desktop (B / CD-ROM), *418 Pages*	Adelstein	400.00
8173667470	Flash Hacks: 100 Industrial Strength Tips & Tools, *504 Pages*	Bhangal	400.00
8173667314	Flash Remoting MX: The Definitive Guide, *652 Pages*	Muck	550.00
8173668590	Flash Out of the Box: A User-Centric Beginner's Guide to Flash (B / CD-ROM), *264 Pages*	Hoekman	300.00
0596002874	Free As In Freedom: Richard Stallman's Crusade for Free Software, *243 Pages*	Williams	750.00
817366868X	GDB Pocket Reference, *78 Pages*	Robbins	75.00
817366949X	Google Hacks: Tips & Tools for Smarter Searching 2/ed, *496 Pages*	Calishain	350.00
8173667136	Google Pocket Guide, *144 Pages*	Calishain	125.00
8173669325	Google: The Missing Manual, *312 Pages*	Milstein	325.00
0596006624	Hackers & Painters: Big Ideas from the Computer Age, *272 Pgs.*	Graham	700.00
8173668256	Hardcore Java, *354 Pages*	Simmons	400.00
8173663424	Hardening Cisco Routers, *196 Pages*	Akin	150.00
8173668213	Hardware Hacking Projects for Geeks, *358 Pages*	Fullam	350.00
8173664668	Head First Design Patterns, *688 Pages*	Sierra	500.00
8173665265	Head First EJB: Passing the Sun Certified Business Component Developer Exam, *744 Pages*	Sierra	450.00
8173666024	Head First Java (Covers Java 5.0) 2/ed, *730 Pages*	Sierra	450.00
817366403X	Head First Servlets & JSP: Passing the Sun Certified Web Component Developer Exam, *666 Pages*	Sierra	600.00
8173669341	Hibernate: A Developer's Notebook, *190 Pages*	Elliott	200.00
8173669260	High Performance Linux Cluster with OSCAR, Rocks, OpenMosix, and MPI, *380 Pages*	Sloan	350.00
8173669023	High Performance MySQL, *304 Pages*	Zawodny	300.00
8173665141	HTML & XHTML: The Definitive Guide, 5/ed, *676 Pages*	Musciano	500.00
8173664323	HTML Pocket Reference, *100 Pages*	Niederst	70.00
8173663165	Home Hacking Projects for Geeks, *346 Pages*	Faulkner	325.00

ISBN	Title	Author	Price
8173669449	Home Networking Annoyances: How to Fix the Most Annoying Things About Your Home Network, 234 Pages	Ivens	250.00
0596008597	Illustrations with Photoshop: A Designer's Notebook, 96 Pages	Rodarmor	775.00
8173665109	Information Architecture for the World Wide Web, 2/ed, 492 Pge	Rosenfeld	400.00
8173669414	Internet Annoyances: How to Fix the Most Annoying Things about Going Online, 266 Pages	Gralla	250.00
8173661057	Internet Core Protocols: The Definitive Guide (B / CD-ROM), 476 Pgs	Hall	375.00
8173660158	Internet in a Nutshell, 456 Pages	Quercia	215.00
8173663378	IP Routing, 244 Pages	Malhotra	200.00
817366448X	IPv6 Essentials, 362 Pages	Hagen	300.00
8173663025	IPv6 Network Administration, 316 Pages	Murphy	325.00
8173667489	IRC Hack: 100 Industrial-Strength Tips & Tools, 442 Pages	Mutton	600.00
8173667373	J2EE Design Patterns, 390 Pages	Crawford	325.00
8173663432	J2ME in a Nutshell: A Desktop Quick Reference, 474 Pages	Topley	400.00
8173669295	Jakarta Commons Cookbook, 412 Pages	O'Brien	375.00
8173669481	Jakarta Struts Cookbook, 536 Pages	Siggelkow	400.00
8173667144	Jakarta Struts Pocket Reference, 142 Pages	Cavaness	125.00
8173668477	Java 1.5 Tiger: A Developer's Notebook, 210 Pages	McLaughlin	175.00
8173664471	Java & SOAP, 286 Pages	Englander	275.00
817366367X	Java & XML, 2/ed, 534 Pages	McLaughlin	450.00
8173664498	Java & XML Data Binding, 224 Pages	McLaughlin	225.00
8173663793	Java & XSLT, 534 Pages	Burke	350.00
8173669368	Java Cookbook (Coverage of 1.5), 2/ed, 872 Pages	Darwin	600.00
8173666660	Java Database Best Practices, 304 Pages	Eckstein	275.00
8173666679	Java Data Objects, 568 Pages	Jordan	350.00
817366577X	Java Enterprise Best Practices, 296 Pages	Eckstein	275.00
8173664625	Java Enterprise in a Nutshell: A Desktop Quick Reference, 2/ed, 1,004 Pages	Farley	600.00
8173662843	Java Examples in a Nutshell 2/ed, 592 Pages	Flanagan	225.00
8173668639	Java Examples in a Nutshell: A Tutorial Companion to Java in a Nutshell, 3/ed, 728 Pages	Flanagan	400.00
8173666687	Java Extreme Programming Cookbook, 296 Pages	Burke	225.00
817366434X	Java in a Nutshell: A Desktop Quick Reference, 4/ed, 1,000 Pgs	Flanagan	600.00
8173664404	Java Management Extensions, 318 Pages	Perry	275.00
8173663211	Java Message Service, 300 Pages	Monson-Haefel	225.00
817366353X	Java Network Programming, 3/ed, 770 Pages	Harold	500.00
8173665117	Java NIO, 308 Pages	Hitchens	275.00
8173665788	Java Performance Tuning, 2/ed, 600 Pages	Shirazi	450.00
8173663904	Java Programming with Oracle JDBC, 504 Pages	Bales	300.00
8173663815	Java RMI, 572 Pages	Grosso	400.00

ISBN	Title	Author	Price
8173664129	Java Security, 2/ed, 624 Pages	Oaks	500.00
8173668221	Java Servlet & JSP Cookbook, 756 Pages	Perry	500.00
8173662851	Java Servlet Programming 2/ed, 786 Pages	Hunter	500.00
8173665680	Java Swing, 2/ed, 1,288 Pages	Loy	750.00
8173665923	Java Threads (Covers J2SE 5.0), 3/ed, 368 Pages	Oaks	300.00
8173663440	Java Web Services, 286 Pages	Chappell	250.00
8173666695	Java Web Services in a Nutshell: A Desktop Quick Reference (Covers J2EE 1.4 & JWSD²). 696 Pages	Topley	500.00
8173669465	**JBoss: A Developer's Notebook, 182 Pages**	**Richards**	**200.00**
8173666709	JavaScript and DHTML Cookbook, 546 Pages	Goodman	475.00
8173663823	JavaScript: The Definitive Guide (Covers JavaScript 1.5), 4/ed, 942 Pages	Flanagan	750.00
8173669031	**JavaServer Faces, 614 Pages**	**Bergsten**	**450.00**
8173665303	JavaServer Pages (Covers JSP 2.0 & JSTL 1.1), 3/ed, 762 Pgs	Bergsten	500.00
8173663831	JavaServer Pages Pocket Reference, 96 Pages	Bergsten	65.00
8173666717	**JDBC Pocket Reference, 160 Pages**	**Bales**	**100.00**
8173668604	JUnit Pocket Guide, 100 Pages	Beck	100.00
059600768X	Just A Geek, 296 Pages	Wheaton	700.00
817366515X	JXTA in a Nutshell: A Desktop Quick Reference, 422 Pages	Oaks	225.00
8173665605	Kerberos: The Definitive Guide, 280 Pages	Garman	275.00
8173669724	**Killer Game Programming in Java, 986 Pages**	**Davison**	**675.00**
8173666725	LDAP System Administration, 318 Pages	Carter	300.00
8173665168	Learning C#, 374 Pages	Liberty	325.00
8173669635	**Learning GNU Emacs, 3/ed, 544 Pages**	**Cameron**	**450.00**
8173663912	Learning Oracle PL/SQL (Covers Oracle9i), 452 Pages	Pribyl	325.00
8173663718	Learning Perl, 3/ed, 344 Pages	Schwartz	275.00
8173667322	Learning PHP 5, 378 Pages	Sklar	350.00
8173667381	Learning Python (Covers Python 2.3), 2/ed, 630 Pages	Lutz	525.00
8173668051	**Learning the Bash Shell, 3/ed, 362 Pages**	**Newham**	**350.00**
8173664447	Learning the Korn Shell, 2/ed, 438 Pages	Rosenblatt	325.00
8173664234	Learning the UNIX Operating System, 5/ed, 174 Pages	Peek	125.00
8173660611	Learning the vi Editor 6/ed, 352 Pages	Lamb	250.00
8173666741	Learning UML, 304 Pages	Si Alhir	150.00
817366563X	Learning Visual Basic .NET, 326 Pages	Liberty	250.00
8173669422	**Learning Windows Server 2003, 682 Pages**	**Hassell**	**525.00**
817366062X	lex & yacc 2/ed, 392 Pages	Levine	225.00
8173668442	**Linux Cookbook, 590 Pages**	**Schroder**	**450.00**
8173668493	**Linux Device Drivers (Covers Version 2.6.10 Linux Kernel), 3/ed, 646 Pages**	**Rubini**	**450.00**
8173667179	Linux in a Nutshell, 4/ed, 994 Pages	Siever	500.00

ISBN	Title	Author	Price
8173669457	Linux in a Windows World, *504 Pages*	Smith	450.00
8173668507	Linux iptables Pocket Reference, *106 Pages*	Purdy	100.00
8173664544	**Linux Network Administrator's Guide, *3/ed, 372 Pages***	Kirch	350.00
8173668647	**Linux Pocket Guide, *212 Pages***	Barrett	150.00
8173667187	Linux Security Cookbook, *340 Pages*	Barrett	325.00
817366675X	Linux Server Hacks: 100 Industrial - Strength Tips & Tools, *240 Pages*	Flickenger	225.00
8173668434	Linux Unwired, *322 Pages*	Weeks	300.00
817366465X	Managing & Using MySQL, *2/ed, 448 Pages*	Reese	325.00
8173662746	Managing IMAP, *412 Pages*	Mullet	200.00
8173660271	Managing IP Networks with Cisco Routers, *352 Pages*	Ballew	200.00
8173663610	Managing NFS & NIS, *2/ed, 518 Pages*	Stern	400.00
8173669589	Managing Projects with GNU Make, *3/ed, 310 Pages*	Mecklenburg	300.00
8173665230	Managing RAID on Linux, *268 Pages*	Vadala	275.00
8173668655	Managing Security with Snort & IDS Tools, *296 Pages*	Cox Ph.D.	300.00
8173662800	Managing the Windows 2000 Registry, *564 Pages*	Robicheaux	325.00
0596007035	Mapping Hacks: Tips & Tools for Electronic Cartography, *574 Pages*	Erle	900.00
8173661162	Mastering Algorithms with C (B / DISK), *572 Pages*	Loudon	400.00
8173664455	**Mastering FreeBSD and OpenBSD Security, *472 Pages***	Korff	425.00
8173664366	Mastering Oracle SQL, (Cover Oracle9i), *348 Pages*	Mishra	225.00
8173664617	**Mastering Oracle SQL (Covers Oracle Database10g), *2/ed, 504 Pages***	Mishra	400.00
8173666768	Mastering Perl for Bioinformatics, *406 Pages*	Tisdall	300.00
8173665087	Mastering Regular Expressions, *2/ed, 492 Pages*	Friedl	400.00
8173665702	Mastering Visual Studio .NET 2003, *420 Pages*	Flanders	375.00
8173667918	**Maven: A Developer's Notebook, *232 Pages***	Massol	250.00
8173667497	Mono: A Developer's Notebook, *312 Pages*	Dumbill	325.00
8173665648	MySQL Cookbook (Covers MySQL 4.0), *1,028 Pages*	DuBois	750.00
817366806X	MySQL in a Nutshell, *358 Pages*	Dyer	325.00
8173666776	**MySQL Pocket Reference, *94 Pages***	Reese	100.00
8173665249	NetBeans: The Definitive Guide, *662 Pages*	Boudreau	500.00
8173668809	Network Security Assessment, *398 Pages*	McNab	325.00
8173668396	**Network Security Tools: Writing, Hacking, and Modifying Security Tools , *350 Pages***	Dhanjani	350.00
8173663521	Networking Security Hacks: 100 Industrial-Strength Tips & Tools, *328 Pages*	Lockhart	325.00
8173663688	Network Troubleshooting Tools, *370 Pages*	Sloan	250.00
8173667926	**Nokia Smartphone Hacks, *418 Pages***	Yuan	400.00
8173667845	NUnit Pocket Reference, *100 Pages*	Hamilton	100.00

ISBN	Title	Author	Price
8173665613	Object-Oriented Programming with Visual Basic .NET, 306 Pages	Hamilton	225.00
8173668264	Office 2003 XML, 596 Pages	Lenz	450.00
8173667519	OpenOffice.org Writer (B / CD-ROM), 234 Pages	Weber	250.00
8173667403	Optimizing Oracle Performance, 426 Pages	Milsap	375.00
8173669287	Oracle Applications Server 10g Essentials, 292 Pages	Greenwald	275.00
8173661170	Oracle Built-in Packages (B / DISK), 956 Pages	Feuerstein	475.00
8173667071	Oracle Data Dictionary Pocket Reference, 150 Pages	Kreines	125.00
8173660670	Oracle Database Administration: The Essential Reference, 552 Pages	Kreines	325.00
817366417X	Oracle DBA Checklist Pocket Reference, 88 Pages	RevealNet	65.00
8173660689	Oracle Distributed Systems (B / DISK), 552 Pages	Dye	325.00
8173664110	Oracle Essentials: Oracle9i, Oracle8i & Oracle8, 2/ed, 382 Pgs.	Greenwald	275.00
817366935X	Oracle Essentials: Oracle Database 10g, 3/ed, 368 Pages	Greenwald	275.00
817366580X	Oracle in a Nutshell: A Desktop Quick Reference, 934 Pages	Greenwald	600.00
8173664560	Oracle Initialization Parameters Pocket Reference (Oracle Database 10g), 128 Pages	Kreines	125.00
8173663246	Oracle Net8 Configuration & Troubleshooting, 412 Pages	Toledo	250.00
8173663629	Oracle PL/SQL Best Practices, 208 Pages	Feuerstein	200.00
8173661189	Oracle PL/SQL Built-ins Pocket Reference, 78 Pages	Feuerstein	60.00
8173665176	Oracle PL/SQL Programming, 3/ed, 1,024 Pages	Feuerstein	600.00
8173662401	Oracle PL/SQL Programming: A Developer's Workbook, 576 Pages	Feuerstein	300.00
8173661197	Oracle PL/SQL Programming: Guide to Oracle8i Features (B / DISK), 264 Pages	Feuerstein	235.00
8173668116	Oracle Regular Expression Pocket Reference, 74 Pages	Burcham	75.00
8173661200	Oracle SAP Administration, 208 Pages	Burleson	275.00
8173660298	Oracle Scripts (B / CD-ROM), 208 Pages	Lomansky	250.00
8173660719	Oracle Security, 448 Pages	Theriault	220.00
8173663637	Oracle SQL* Loader: The Definitive Guide, 278 Pages	Gennick	175.00
8173669333	**Oracle SQL*Plus Pocket Reference, 3/ed, 160 Pages**	**Gennick**	**125.00**
8173666067	**Oracle SQL*Plus: The Definitive Guide, 2/ed, 592 Pages**	**Gennick**	**400.00**
8173662916	Oracle SQL: The Essential Reference, 424 Pages	Kreines	250.00
8173661847	**Oracle Utilities Pocket Reference, 136 Pages**	**Mishra**	**100.00**
8173661219	Oracle Web Applications: PL/SQL Developer's Intro, 264 Pages	Odewahn	180.00
817366028X	Oracle8 Design Tips, 136 Pages	Ensor	120.00
8173668027	PC Annoyances: How to Fix the Most Annoying Thingsabout your Personal Computer, 236 Pages	Bass	225.00
8173667152	PC Hacks: 100 Industrial-Strength Tips & Tools, 316 Pages	Aspinwall	300.00

ISBN	Title	Author	Price
8173669732	PC Hardware Annoyances: How to Fix the Most ANNOYING Things About Your Computer Hardware, 276 Pages	Bigelow	275.00
817366532X	PC Hardware in a Nutshell: A Desktop Quick Reference, 3/ed, 848 Pages	Thompson	325.00
8173667128	PDF Hacks: 100 Industrial-Strength Tips & Tools, 308 Pages	Steward	300.00
8173664463	Perl & XML, 224 Pages	Ray	175.00
8173661073	Perl 5 Pocket Reference, 3/ed, 96 Pages	Vromans	70.00
8173667195	Perl 6 Essentials, 208 Pages	Randal	175.00
8173668280	**Perl Best Practices, 554 Pages**	Conway	425.00
8173667330	Perl Cookbook, 2/ed, 976 Pages	Christiansen	675.00
8173668043	Perl Template Toolkit, 600 Pages	Chamberlain	525.00
8173665710	PHP Cookbook, 638 Pages	Sklar	550.00
0596008600	Photo Retouching with Photoshop: A Designer's Notebook, 96 Pages	CLEC'H	775.00
817366871X	Postfix: The Definitive Guide, 288 Pages	Dent	275.00
8173669805	**Powerpoint 2003 PersonalTrainer (B / CD-ROM), (2 Color book) 342 Pages**	CustomGuide	425.00
8173660301	Practical C Programming 3/ed, 456 Pages	Oualline	225.00
8173666822	Practical C++ Programming, 2/ed, 582 Pages	Oualline	225.00
817366711X	Practical mod_perl, 932 Pages	Bekman	675.00
8173663920	Practical PostgreSQL (B / CD-ROM), 642 Pages	Command Prompt Inc.	450.00
8173666733	Practical RDF, 360 Pages	Powers	450.00
8173666830	Practical Unix & Internet Security, 3/ed, 994 Pages	Garfinkel	650.00
8173664390	Practical VoIP Using VOCAL, 532 Pages	Dang	450.00
8173665818	Programming .NET 1.1 Components, 488 Pages	Lowy	375.00
8173667209	Programming .NET Security, 704 Pages	Freeman	550.00
8173667411	Programming .NET Windows Applications (Covers .NET 1.1, & Visual Studio .NET 2003), 1316 Pages	Liberty	750.00
8173664382	Programming .NET Web Services, 500 Pages	Ferrara	375.00
817366742X	Programming ASP .NET (Covers .NET 1.1, & Visual Studio .NET 2003), 2/ed, 1026 Pages	Liberty	675.00
8173669651	**Programming C# (Covers C# 2.0, .NET 2.0 & Visual Studio 2005), 4/ed, 680 Pages**	Liberty	525.00
817366076X	Programming Embedded Systems in C & C++, 198 Pages	Barr	150.00
8173669694	**Programming Flash Communication Server, 842 Pages**	Lesser	600.00
8173661278	Programming Internet E-mail, 384 Pages	Wood	225.00
8173668183	Programming Jakarta Struts 2/ed, 470 Pages	Cavaness	400.00
8173662657	Programming Perl 3/ed, 1,116 Pages	Wall	675.00
8173663114	Programming PHP, 530 Pages	Lerdorf	350.00

ISBN	Title	Author	Price
8173667500	Programming Python (Covers Python 2) (B / CD-ROM), 2/ed, 1,305 Pages	Lutz	750.00
8173662371	Programming the Perl DBI, 372 Pages	Descartes	200.00
8173667063	Programming Visual Basic .NET 2003, 2/ed, 564 Pages	Liberty	425.00
8173665737	Programming Web Services with Perl, 492 Pages	Ray	400.00
8173662045	Programming Web Services with SOAP, 268 Pages	Snell	200.00
817366207X	Programming Web Services with XML-RPC, 240 Pages	St.Laurent	175.00
8173668175	Programming with QT (Covers Qt 3), 2/ed, 532 Pages	Dalheimer	450.00
817366479X	**Python Cookbook (Covers Python 2.3 & 2.4), 2/ed, 852 Pgs**	**Martelli**	**600.00**
8173669708	**Python Pocket Reference (Covers Python 2.4), 3/ed, 168 Pgs**	**Lutz**	**125.00**
8173666857	Python in a Nutshell: A Desktop Quick Reference (Cover Python 2.2), 662 Pages	Martelli	500.00
8173668485	qmail, 268 Pages	Levine	275.00
817366689X	Real World Web Services, 230 Pages	Iverson	225.00
8173667276	Regular Expression Pocket Reference, 112 Pages	Stubblebine	100.00
0596007191	Revolution in the Valley, 324 Pages	Hertzfeld	775.00
8173665206	Running Linux, 4/ed, 702 Pages	Welsh	425.00
8173667055	Samba Pocket Reference, 2/ed, 146 Pages	Eckstein	125.00
8173664226	SAX2 (Simple API for XML), 248 Pages	Brownell	175.00
8173667217	Secure Coding: Principles & Practices, 200 Pages	Graff	225.00
8173667284	Secure Programming Cookbook for C and C++, 800 Pages	Viega	600.00
817366840X	Security Warrior, 562 Pages	Peikari	500.00
ō173663262	Securing Windows NT/2000 Servers for the Internet, 200 Pages	Norberg	125.00
8173669376	Securing Windows Server 2003, 456 Pages	Danseglio	400.00
8173660786	sed & awk, 2/ed, 440 Pages	Dougherty	300.00
817366918X	SELINUX NSA's Open Source Security Enhanced Linux, 264 Pgs	McCarty	275.00
8173665834	sendmail, 3/ed, 1,238 Pages	Costales	850.00
817366823X	sendmail Cookbook, 418 Pages	Hunt	400.00
8173666865	Sequence Analysis in a Nutshell: A Guide to Common Tools and Databases (Covers EMBOSS 2.5.0), 310 Pages	Markel	275.00
8173664161	Server Load Balancing, 198 Pages	Bourke	150.00
817366739X	**SharePoint User's Guide, 158 Pages**	**IDC**	**150.00**
817366983X	**SharePoint Office Pocket Guide, 94 Pages**	**Webb**	**75.00**
8173669503	Snort Cookbook, 296 Pages	Orebaugh	300.00
8173663866	Solaris 8 Administrator's Guide, 308 Pages	Watters	225.00
8173669198	SpamAssassin (Covers 3.0), 232 Pages	Schwartz	250.00
8173668191	Spidering Hacks: 100 Industrial - Strength Tips & Tools, 436 Pgs	Hemenway	350.00
817366837X	**Spring: A Developer's Notebook, 202 Pages**	**Tate**	**200.00**
8173666520	SQL in a Nutshell (Covers SQL Server, DB2, MySQL, Oracle & PostgreSQL), 2/ed, 720 Pages	Kline	450.00

ISBN	Title	Author	Price
8173667438	SQL Pocket Reference (Cover Oracle. DB2, SQL Server & MySQL), 170 Pages	Gennick	125.00
8173668248	SQL Tunning (Covers Oracle, DB2 & SQL Server), 356 Pages	Tow	325.00
8173668418	Squid: The Definitive Guide, 472 Pages	Wessels	450.00
8173662924	SSH: The Secure Shell: The Definitive Guide, 564 Pages	Barrett	325.00
8173668574	STL Pocket Reference, 136 Pages	Lischner	100.00
8173669511	SWT: A Developer's Notebook, 330 Pages	Hatton	325.00
8173664811	Swing Hacks, 554 Pages	Marinacci	425.00
8173665311	Switching to VoIP, 514 Pages	Wallingford	450.00
8173663254	T1: A Survival Guide, 224 Pages	Gast	225.00
817366093X	Tcl/Tk in a Nutshell: A Desktop Quick Reference, 480 Pages	Raines	240.00
8173664676	TCP/IP Network Administration 3/ed, 756 Pages	Hunt	500.00
8173666512	Test Driving Linux: A Desktop User's Guide (B / CD-ROM), 372 Pages	Lavigna	350.00
8173666873	Tomcat: The Definitive Guide (Cover Tomcat 4), 336 Pages	Brittain	300.00
8173660352	UML in a Nutshell: A Desktop Quick Reference, 336 Pages	Alhir	225.00
8173667225	UML Pocket Reference, 96 Pages	Pilone	100.00
8173665893	Understanding the Linux Kernel, 2/ed, 832 Pages	Bovet	500.00
817366627X	Unit Test Frameworks (B / CD-ROM), 222 Pages	Hamill	225.00
8173661324	UNIX in a Nutshell: A Desktop Quick Reference for SVR4 & Solaris 7, 3/ed, 628 Pages	Robbins	325.00
8173665656	Unix Power Tools, 3/ed, 1,162 Pages	Powers	750.00
8173666202	Upgrading to PHP 5 (Covers MySQL 4.1), 358 Pages	Trachtenberg	350.00
8173660948	Using & Managing PPP, 464 Pages	Sun	240.00
8173665842	Using Samba, 2/ed, 570 Pages	Eckstein	500.00
8173664374	VB .NET Core Classes in a Nutshell: A Desktop Quick Reference (B / CD-ROM), 584 Pages	Kurniawan	500.00
817366594X	VB .NET Language Pocket Reference, 160 Pages	Roman	125.00
8173666881	VBScript in a Nutshell: A Desktop Quick Reference, 2/e, 528 Pages	Lomax	400.00
8173663300	VBScript Pocket Referenoe, 118 Pages	Childs	60.00
8173668582	Version Control With Subversion, 332 Pages	Collins - Sussman	350.00
8173662622	vi Editor Pocket Reference, 76 Pages	Robbins	60.00
8173661340	Virtual Private Networks, 2/ed, 228 Pages	Scott	150.00
8173666164	Visual Basic 2005: A Developer's Notebook, 272 Pages	MacDonald	250.00
8173669740	Visual C# 2005: A Developer's Notebook, 250 Pages	Liberty	225.00
8173660964	Visual Basic Controls in a Nutshell, 512 Pages	Dictor	310.00
817366501X	Visual Studio Hacks: Tips & Tools for Turbocharging the IDE, 304 Pages	Avery	375.00
8173668094	Volume One: Xlib Programming Manual (Version 11), 824 Pages	Nye	575.00

ISBN	Title	Author	Price
8173668108	Volume Two: Xlib Reference Manual (Version 11), 3/ed, 948 Pages	Nye	600.00
8173668086	Volume Zero: X Protocol Reference Manual (Version X11), 468 Pgs.	Nye	350.00
8173668310	X Windows Reference Manaul (3 Volume Set)	Nye	1,350.00
0596007337	We the Media: Grassroots Journalism by the People, for the People, 320 Pages	Gillmor	775.00
8173663092	WebLogic 8.1: The Definitive Guide, 860 Pages	Mountjoy	600.00
8173669058	**Web Database Application with PHP & MySQL (Covers PEAR, PHP 5 & MySQL 4.1), 2/ed, 828 Pages**	**Willaims**	**600.00**
8173663750	Web Design in a Nutshell: A Desktop Quick Reference, 2/ed, 656 Pages	Niederst	425.00
8173664412	Web Performance Tuning, 2/ed, 488 Pages	Killelea	350.00
8173665214	Web Privacy with P3P, 350 Pages	Cranor	425.00
8173663947	Web Security, Privacy & Commerce, 2/ed, 768 Pages	Garfinkel	500.00
8173663394	Web Services Essentials, 320 Pages	Cerami	200.00
8173665931	WebLogic Server 6.1 Workbook for Enterprise JavaBeans, 3/ed, 264 Pages	Nyberg	200.00
8173661308	The Whole Internet: The Next Generation, 576 Pages	Conner/Krol	425.00
8173661367	Win32 API Programming with Visual Basic (B / CD-ROM), 534 Pages	Roman	400.00
8173662789	Windows 2000 Administration in a Nutshell: A Desktop Quick Reference, 1000 Pages	Tulloch	350.00
8173663319	Windows 2000 Commands Pocket Reference, 122 Pages	Frisch	60.00
8173660743	Windows 2000 Quick Fixes, 304 Pages	Boyce	225.00
8173660883	Windows NT TCP/IP Network Administration, 512 Pages	Hunt	250.00
8173666903	Windows Server 2003 in a Nutshell: A Desktop Quick Reference, 672 Pages	Tulloch	550.00
8173668833	Windows Server Hacks: 100 Industrial-Strength Tips & Tools , 328 Pages	Tulloch	325.00
8173667454	Windows XP Hacks: 100 Industrial-Strength Tips & Tools, 294 Pgs	Gralla	350.00
8173663564	Windows XP in a Nutshell: A Desktop Quick Reference, 640 Pages	Karp	375.00
8173669643	**Windows XP Personal Trainer (B / CD-ROM), 480 Pages**	**CustomGuide**	**550.00**
8173666911	Windows XP Pocket Reference, 196 Pages	Karp	125.00
8173665915	Windows XP Unwired: A Guide for Home, Office, and the Road, 316 Pages	Lee	275.00
8173667462	Wireless Hacks: 100 Industrial-Strength Tips & Tools, 424 Pgs.	Flickenger	275.00
8173662770	Word 2000 in a Nutshell: A Power User's Quick Reference, 516 Pgs.	Glenn	225.00
817366692X	Word Pocket Guide, 160 Pages	Glenn	125.00
8173665354	Writing Excel Macros with VBA, 2/ed, 580 Pages	Roman	450.00

ISBN	Title	Author	Price
8173660778	Writing Word Macros, 416 Pages	Roman	275.00
8173668450	XML in a Nutshell (Covers XML 1.1 & XInclude), 3/ed, 724 Pages	Harold	500.00
8173666156	XML Hacks: 100 Industrial-Strength Tips & Tools, 490 Pages	Fitzgerald	425.00
8173663343	XML Pocket Reference, 2/ed, 128 Pages	Eckstein	100.00

FORTHCOMING TITLES

August 2005

ISBN	Title	Author	Price
8173664587	ASP .NET 2.0: Developer's Notebook, 358 Pages	Lee	325.00
8173661995	Access 2003 Personal Trainer (B / CD-ROM), (2 Color book), 372 Pages	CustomGuide	400.00
0596100965	Adobe Photoshop CS2 One-on-One (B / DVD), 476 Pages	McClelland	1,900.00
8173667721	Car PC Hacks: Tips & Tools for Geeking Your Ride, 394 Pages	Stolarz	400.00
8173667799	Computer Privacy Annoyances, 218 Pages	Tynan	225.00
8173664633	Firefox Hacks, 398 Pages	McFarlane	350.00
8173667861	Home Networking: The Missing Manual, 263 Pages	Lowe	275.00
8173670161	Learning Java (B/CD-ROM), 3/ed, 946 Pages	Niemeyer	600.00
8173664684	Linux Desktop Hacks: Tips & Tools for Customizing and Optimizing your OS, 384 Pages	Petreley	350.00
8173668272	PC Pest Control, 298 Pages	Gralla	300.00
8173668361	Perl Testing: A Developer's Notebook, 218 Pages	Langworth	225.00
8173668426	QuickTime for Java: A Developer's Notebook, 266 Pages	Adamson	275.00
8173666032	TOAD Pocket Reference for Oracle, 2/ed, 126 Pages	McGrath	125.00
8173666172	Windows Server Cookbook: For Windows Server 2003 & Windows 2000, 706 Pages	Allen	550.00
8173669716	Word 2003 Personal Trainer (B / CD-ROM), 462 Pages	CustomGuide	450.00
8173666113	Word Annoyances, 218 Pages	Hart	225.00

September 2005

ISBN	Title	Author	Price
817367017X	Cisco IOS in a Nutshell, 2/ed, 808 Pages	Boney	500.00
059600849X	Commercial Photoshop Retouching: In The Studio, 410 Pgs	Honiball	2,000.00
8173670196	Creating Microsoft SharePoint Sites, 314 Pages	Webb	300.00
817367020X	Digital Identity, 274 Pages	Windley	1,600.00
0596100159	Digital Photography Pocket Guide, 3/ed, 160 Pages	Story	700.00
8173670226	Eclipse IDE Pocket Guide, 140 Pages	Burnette	125.00
8173670234	Essential Business Process Modeling, 346 Pages	Havey	325.00
8173670250	Open Source for the Enterprise, 246 Pages	Woods	325.00
8173670269	Open Sources 2.0, 314 Pages	DiBona	325.00
8173670277	Oracle DBA Pocket Guide, 128 Pages	Kreines	125.00
8173670285	RT Essentials, 234 Pages	Vincent	225.00
8173670293	Security and Usability, 600 Pages	Cranor	500.00
8173670307	XSLT 1.0 Pocket Reference, 116 Pages	Lenz	100.00

ISBN	Title	Author	Price
	October 2005		
8173670315	Access Annoyances: How to Avoid the Most Annoying Things About Your Favorite Database , 314 Pages	Mitchell	325.00
8173670323	Access for Rookies: The Missing Manual, 314 Pages	Palmer	300.00
8173670331	Asterisk: The Future of Telephony, 514 Pages	Smith	450.00
817367034X	Beyond Java, 170 Pages	Tate	175.00
8173670358	Designing Interfaces, 384 Pages	Tidwell	350.00
8173670366	Essentail PHP Security, 310 Pages	Shiflett	300.00
8173670374	Excel for Rookies: The Missing Manual, 314 Pages	MacDonald	300.00
8173670382	Learning SQL, 410 Pages	Beaulieu	350.00
8173670390	Linux Desktop Pocket Reference, 154 Pages	Brickner	125.00
0596100302	Photoshop Retouching Cookbook for Digital Photographers, 176 Pages	Huggins	1,400.00
8173670412	Prefactoring, 200 Pages	Pugh	200.00
8173670420	Programming Apache Axis, 410 Pages	Haddad	400.00
8173670439	Programming Visual Basic 2005, 800 Pages	Liberty	500.00
8173670447	Visual Basic 2005 Jumpstart Pocket Guide, 164 Pages	Lee	125.00
	November 2005		
8173670455	Blackberry Hacks, 256 Pages	Mabe	275.00
8173670463	Integrating Excel and Access, 514 Pages	Schmalz	425.00
8173670471	Internet Forensics, 304 Pages	Jones	325.00
817367048X	PHP in a Nutshell, 314 Pages	Hudson	300.00
0596100221	Photoshop Photo Effects Cookbook, 176 Pages	Shelbournce	1,400.00
0596008511	Photoshop RAW, 266 Pages	Aaland	1,600.00
817367051X	Powerpoint Annoyances, 266 Pages	Swinford	250.00
8173670528	Practical Development Environments, 352 Pages	Doar	350.00
8173670536	Programming Avalon (B / CD - ROM), 410 Pages	Sells	400.00
8173670544	Producing Free Software, 266 Pages	Fogel	275.00
8173670552	Twisted Network Programming Essentials, 210 Pages	Fettig	225.00
8173670560	Yahoo ! Hacks, 362 Pages	Bausch	325.00
	December 2005		
8173670579	JBoss at Work: A Practical Guide, 256 Pages	Marrs	250.00
8173670587	Oracle PL/SQL for DBAs, 466 Pages	Feuerstein	425.00
8173670595	Programming SQL Server 2005, 362 Pages	Wildermuth	325.00
	February 2006		
8173670609	Bonjour: The Definitive Guide, 256 Pages	Steinberg	275.00
8173670617	C in a Nutshell, 400 Pages	Prinz	275.00

ISBN	Title	Author	Price
8173670625	Firewall Warrior, 610 Pages	Artymiak	500.00
8173670633	JUnit: The Definitive Guide, 310 Pages	Lane	300.00

Shroff / Object Sources

PUBLISHED TITLES

8173668760	Struts Survival Guide: Basics to Best Practices, 224 Pages	Shenoy	225.00

FORTHCOMING TITLES

8173668779	J2EE Project Survival Guide Volume 1		
8173668787	J2EE Project Survival Guide Volume 2		

Shroff / Pearson Education

8129703769	.NET - A Complete Development Cycle (B / CD-ROM), 584 Pages	Lenz	600.00
8129703882	Applying Enterprise JavaBeans: Component-Based Development for the J2EE Platform, 2/ed, 486 Pages	Matena	375.00
8129703777	ASP .NET Solutions - 23 Case Studies, 894 Pages	Leinecker	725.00

Shroff / Rampant TechPress

PUBLISHED TITLES

8173669112	Conducting the J2EE Job Interview: IT Manager Guide for J2EE with Interview Questions, 244 Pages	Hunter	250.00
8173669147	Conducting the Java Job Interview: IT Manager Guide for Java with Interview Questions, 308 Pages	Hunter	300.00
8173669155	Conducting the Network Administrator Job Interview: IT Manager Guide with Cisco CCNA Job Interview Questions, 146 Pages	Haeder	150.00
8173667764	Conducting the Oracle Job Interview Tips - IT Manager Guide for Oracle Job Interviews with Interview Questions (Includes Oracle 9i), 144 Pages	Ault	150.00
8173669139	Conducting the Programmer Job Interview: IT Manager Guide with Java, J2EE, C, C++, Unix, PHP and Oracle Interview Questions!, 308 Pages	Burleson	300.00
8173669074	Conducting the UNIX Job Interview: IT Manager Guide with Unix Interview Questions, 180 Pages	Haeder	200.00
8173667829	Conducting the Web Designer Job Interview: IT Manager J2EE Job Interview Questions, 308 Pages	Burleson	300.00
8173669082	Conducting the Web Master Job Interview: IT Manager Guide with Webmaster Interview Questions!, 372 Pages	Burleson	350.00
817366773X	Creating a Self-Tuning Oracle Database - Automating Oracle9i Dynamic SGA Performance, 156 Pages	Burleson	150.00
8173664927	Easy Oracle Automatic: Oracle10g Automatic Storage, Memory and Diagnostic Features, 300 Pages	Dr. Kumar	300.00

ISBN	Title	Author	Price
8173667810	Mike Ault's Oracle Internals Monitoring & Tuning Scripts - Advanced Internals & OCP Certification Insights for the Master DBA (Includes Oracle 10g), 368 Pages	Ault	350.00
8173668523	OCP Instructor's Guide for Oracle DBA Certification: A Study Guide to Advanced Oracle Certified Professional Database Administration Techniques, 340 Pages	Foot	325.00
817366854X	Oracle10g Grid & Real Application Clusters: Oracle10g Grid Computing with RAC, 868 Pages	Ault	600.00
8173668558	Oracle Database 10g New Features: Oracle10g Reference for Advanced Tuning & Administration, 548 Pages	Ault	450.00
8173664919	Oracle Dataguard: Standby Database Failover Handbook, 364 Pgs	Kumar	325.00
8173669104	Oracle Disk I / O Tuning: Disk IO Performance & Optimization for Oracle 10g Database, 244 Pages	Ault	250.00
8173667748	Oracle Performance Troubleshooting – with Dictionary Internals SQL & Tuning Scripts (Includes Oracle 9i), 268 Pages	Schumacher	250.00
8173668515	Oracle Privacy Security Auditing: Includes Federal Law Compliance with HIPAA, Sarbanes-Oxley & The Gramm-Leach-Bliley Act GLB (Includes Oracle 10g), 692 Pages	Nanda	575.00
8173667756	Oracle9i RAC - Oracle Real Application Clusters Configuration and Internals, 628 Pages	Ault	500.00
8173667780	Oracle Replication - Snapshot, Multi-Master & Materialized Views Scripts (Includes Oracle 10g), 244 Pages	Garmany	250.00
8173669546	Oracle Solid State Disk Tuning: High Performance Oracle Tuning with RAM Disk, 204 Pages	Burleson	200.00
8173669090	Oracle SQL Tuning & CBO Internals (Includes Oracle 10g), 354 Pages	Floss	350.00
8173664994	Oracle Streams: High Speed Replication & Data Sharing, 308 Pgs	Tumma	300.00
8173667772	Oracle Utilities - Using Hidden Programs, Import / Export, SQL*Loader, Oradebug, Dbverify, Tkprof & More (Includes Oracle 9i), 276 Pages	Moore	250.00
8173664978	Oracle Wait Event Tuning: High Performance with Wait Event Interface Analysis (Includes Oracle 10g), 276 Pages	Andert	275.00
8173669120	Top Answers to Job Interview Questions: Includes questions you must ask at every interview, 148 Pages	Burleson	150.00

ISBN	Title	Author	Price

FORTHCOMING TITLES

August 2005

ISBN	Title	Author	Price
8173664854	Conducting the Web Services Job Interview: IT Manager Guide for Web Services Job Interviews with Delphi, .Net, XML UDDI, SOAP, ASP .NET & WSL Web Services Job Interview Questions, 256 Pages	Brown	250.00
8173664900	Conducting the Windows Advanced Server Job Interview: IT Manager Guide to Windows Advanced Server Job Interviews with Itanium, .NET & Windows Advanced Server Oracle Job Interview Questions, 276 Pages	Burleson	275.00
8173669872	Easy Linux Commands: Working Examples of Linux Command Syntax, 250 Pages	Clark	250.00
8173669902	Easy Oracle Jumpstart: Oracle Database Management Concepts &Administration (Includes 10g), 200 Pages	Freeman	200.00
8173664935	Easy Oracle PL/SQL Programming: Get Started Fast with Working PL/SQL Code Examples (Includes 10g), 200 Pgs.	Col. Garmany	200.00
8173669813	Easy Oracle SQL: Get Started Fast Writing SQL Reports with SQL*Plus, 200 Pages	Col. Garmany	200.00
8173669821	Oracle Job Scheduling: Creating Robust Task Management with dbms_job and Oracle 10g dbms_Scheduler, 240 Pages	Dr. Hall	225.00
8173669910	Oracle RAC & Grid Tuning with Solid - State Disk: Experts Secrets for High Performance Clustered Grid Computing (Includes 10g), 230 Pages	Ault	225.00
8173669538	Oracle Silver Bullets: Real - World Oracle Performance Secrets, 200 Pages	Burleson	200.00
8173669856	Oracle Tuning: Oracle Time - Series Optimization with the Automatic Workload Repository, 640 Pages	Burleson	500.00
817366661X	Oracle Tuning Power Scripts with 100+ High Performance SQL Scripts, 300 Pages	Ault	300.00
8173669937	You're Fired! Firing Computer Professionals: The IT Manager Guide for Terminating "With Cause", 240 Pages	Papaj	250.00

September 2005

ISBN	Title	Author	Price
8173669848	Easy Java Debugging: Java Testing & Development for Speed & Quality, 240 Pages	Gradner	250.00
8173669945	High Performance SQL Server DBA Tuning & Optimization Secrets (Splash "SQL Server 2005 Yukon"), 240 Pages	Schumacher	250.00
8173669953	Super SQL Server Systems: Turbocharge Database Performance with C++ External Procedures, 450 Pages	Gamma	400.00

ISBN	Title	Author	Price
8173665184	Black Hat Physical Device Security: Exploting Hardware and Software, 422 Pages	Miller	400.00
8173665877	Buffer OverFlow Attacks: Defect, Exploit, Prevent, 526 Pgs.	Foster	475.00
8173667896	Building A Cisco Wireless LAN, 532 Pages	Ouellet	450.00
8173667969	Building DMZS for Enterprise Network, 832 Pages	Schmied	600.00
8173667527	Building SANs With Brocade Fabric Switches, 480 Pages	Judd	400.00
8173667934	Check Point NG / AI:Next Generation with Application Intelligence Security Administration, 628 Pages	Tobkin	525.00
8173667616	Cisco Security Professional's Guide to Secure Intrusion Detection Systems, 676 Pages	Baumrucker	550.00
8173667535	Cisco Security Specialist's Guide to PIX Firewall, 608 Pages	Osipov	525.00
8173666253	Configuring and Troubleshooting Windows XP Professional (B / CD-ROM), 818 Pages	Grasdal	600.00
8173666245	Configuring Cisco Voice Over IP, 2/ed, 578 Pages	Flannagan	450.00
8173665826	Configuring NetScreen Firewalls, 740 Pages	Cameron	550.00
8173667578	Configuring Symantec AntiVirus: Corporate Edition, 756 Pages	Hunter	600.00
8173668957	CYA Securing Exchange Server 2003 & Outlook Web Access, 340 Pages	Walther	400.00
8173658965	CYA Securing IIS 6.0, 424 Pages	Cheah	425.00
8173665044	Cyber Adversary Characterization: Auditing the Hacker Mind, 512 Pages	Parker	375.00
8173669961	Cyber Spying: Tracking Your Family's (Sometimes) Secret Online Lives, 470 Pages	Fair	475.00
8173666237	Dr. Tom Shinder's ISA Server and Beyond (B / CD-ROM), 866 Pages	Shinder	600.00
8173665060	Deploying Citrix MetaFrame Presentation Server 3.0 with Windows Server 2003 Terminal Services, 600 Pages	Wilson	500.00
817366787X	Designing a Wireless Network, 410 Pages	Wheat	350.00
8173668752	Ethereal Packet Sniffing (B / CD-ROM), 510 Pages	Orebaugh	475.00
8173666105	Google Hacking for Penetration Testers, 532 Pages	Long	400.00
817366790X	Hack Proofing Your Wireless Network, 514 Pages	Barnes	450.00
8173665850	Hacking a Terror Network: The Silent Threat of Covert Channels (B / CD-ROM), 406 Pages	Rogers	425.00
8173668922	Hacking the Code: ASP .NET Web Application Security, 474 Pgs.	Burnett	450.00
8173668744	Hardware Hacking, 566 Pages	Grand	500.00
8173669562	How to Cheat at Managing Microsoft Windows Small Business Server 2003, 504 Pages	Snedaker	500.00

ISBN	Title	Author	Price
8173666636	Infosec Career Hacking: Sell Your Skillz, Not Your Soul, *480 Pages*	Bayles	425.00
8173665869	Inside the SPAM Cartel: Trade Secrets From The Dark Side, *436 Pages*	Spammer - X	425.00
8173665079	Intrusion Prevention and Active Response: Deploying Network and Host IPS , *432 Pages*	Rash	400.00
8173668914	Managing and Securing a Cisco Structured Wireless-Aware Network, *500 Pages*	Wall	475.00
8173667888	Managing Cisco Network Security, 2/ed, *784 Pages*	Knipp	600.00
8173667705	MCSA/MCSE (Exam 70-290) Managing and Maintaining a Windows Server 2003 Environment: Study Guide & DVD Training System (B / DVD), *1,028 Pages*	Todd	750.00
8173667659	MCSA/MCSE (Exam 70-291) Implementing, Managing, and Maintaining a Windows Server 2003 Network Infrastructure: Study Guide & DVD Training System (B / DVD), *1,076 Pgs.*	Snedaker	750.00
8173667675	MCSA/MCSE (Exam 70-292): Managing and Maintaining a Windows Server 2003 Environment for an MCSA Certified on Windows 2000 Study Guide & DVD Training System (B / DVD), *739 Pages*	Schmied	600.00
8173667640	MCSE (Exam 70-293) Planning and Maintaining a Windows Server 2003 Network Infrastructure: Study Guide & DVD Training System (B / DVD), *1,120 Pages*	Cross	800.00
8173667632	MCSE (Exam 70-294) Planning, Implementing, and Maintaining a Windows Server 2003 Active Directory Infrastructure: Study Guide & DVD Training System (B / DVD), *1,068 Pages*	Cross	750.00
8173667683	MCSE (Exam 70-296) Planning, Implementing and Maintaining a Windows Server 2003 Environment for an MCSE Certified on Windows 2000: Study Guide & DVD Training System (B / DVD), *848 Pages*	Hunter	700.00
8173667713	MCSE (Exam 70-297) Designing a Windows Server 2003 Active Directory and Network Infrastructure: Study Guide & DVD Training System (B / DVD), *688 Pages*	Barber	600.00
8173667667	MCSE (Exam 70-298) Designing Security for a Windows Server 2003 Network: Study Guide & DVD Training System (B / DVD), *818 Pages*	Khnaser	650.00
8173667594	MCSE / MCSA (Exam 70-214) Implementing & Administering Security in a Windows 2000 Network: Study Guide & DVD Training Systems (B / DVD), *866 Pages*	Schmied	600.00

ISBN	Title	Author	Price
817366997X	Microsoft Log Parser Toolkit, 470 Pages	Giuseppini	450.00
8173665338	Nessus Network Auditing (B / CD-ROM), 548 Pages	Beale	550.00
8173665745	Programmer's Ultimate Security DeskRef, 612 Pages	Foster	525.00
8173667586	Rick Gallaher's MPLS Training Guide: Building Multi Protocol Label Switching Networks, 324 Pages	Gallaher	300.00
8173668868	Security Sage's Guide to Hardening the Network Infrastructure, 546 Pages	Andrés	450.00
8173667942	Security+ Study Guide & DVD Training System (B / DVD), 866 Pages	Cross	650.00
8173668701	Security Assessment: Case Studies for Implementing the NSA IAM, 468 Pages	Miles	425.00
8173668949	Snort 2.1 Intrusion Detection, 2/ed, (B / CD-ROM) 790 Pages	Alder	650.00
8173667551	SSCP Study Guide and DVD Training System (B / DVD), 784 Pages	Jacob	600.00
8173665095	**Sockets, Shellcode, Porting, and Coding: Reverse Engineering Exploits and Tool Coding for Security Professionals, 704 Pages**	Foster	550.00
817366756X	Stealing the Network: How to Own the Box, 330 Pages	Russell	300.00
8173668930	Stealing the Network: How to Own a Continent, 424 Pages	Rogers	450.00
8173668841	WarDriving: Drive, Detect, Defend: A Guide to Wireless Security, 524 Pages	Hurley	400.00
8173665575	Windows to Linux Migration Toolkit (B / CD-ROM), 532 Pages	Allen	475.00
8173665699	Wireless Hacking: Projects for Wi - Fi Enthusiasts, 364 Pages	Barken	375.00

FORTHCOMING TITLES

August 2005

ISBN	Title	Author	Price
8173666962	Cisco PIX Firewalls: Configure / Manage / Troubleshoot, 608 Pages	Khan	500.00
8173667160	Cisco Voice Over IP Security, 608 Pages	Dugan	500.00
8173667349	Dr. Tom Shinder's Configuring ISA Server 2004, 608 Pages	Shinder	500.00
8173667624	Network + Study Guide & Practice Exams: The Gold Standard of Certification Prep, 848 Pages	Honick	600.00
8173665907	Penetration Testing with Google Hacks, 304 Pages	Long	300.00
8173667691	Stealing the Network: How to Own an Identity, 450 Pages	Mullen	400.00

September 2005

ISBN	Title	Author	Price
8173670684	How to Cheat at IT Project Management: Clear, Concise, Easy-To-Read to Effective IT Project Management, 416 Pages	Snedakar	400.00
8173670692	Nessus, Snort, & Ethereal Power Tools: Customizing Open Source Security Applications, 400 Pgs	Caswell	375.00
8173670706	Software Piracy Exposed, 400 Pgs	Honick	400.00

October 2005

ISBN	Title	Author	Price
8173670714	Configuring Check Point NGX VPN-1/Firewall-1, 608 Pages	Stiefel	500.00
8173670722	RFID Security, 448 Pages	Lindstrom	450.00

ISBN	Title	Author	Price
817367003X	Securing IM and P2P Applications for the Enterprise, 650 Pages	Sachs	550.00

Thomson Learning / Autodesk Press

ISBN	Title	Author	Price
0766837831	3D Studio Max 4 Ground Rules (B / CD-ROM), 638 Pages	Peterson	850.00
0766812340	AutoCAD 2000: A Problem-Solving Approach (B / CD-ROM), 1,262 Pages	Tickoo	200.00
0766838471	AutoCAD 2002 for Architecture, 1,040 Pages	Jefferis	200.00
076683851X	AutoCAD 2002: 3D Modeling - A Visual Approach (B / CD-ROM), 644 Pages	Wilson	200.00
0766838536	AutoCAD 2002: A Problem-Solving Approach, 1,127 Pages	Tickoo	200.00
0766842533	AutoCAD 2002: Complete (B / CD-ROM), 840 Pages	Burchard	200.00
0766843696	AutoCAD 2002 Professional (B / CD-ROM), 370 Pages	Burchard	200.00
9812542604	AutoCAD 2004 for Architecture, 942 Pages	Jefferis	675.00
0619130598	CCNA CertBlaster Studennt Edition for Cisco Certified Network Associate (CCNA) Exam # 640-607 (CD-ROM Only)	Thomson	525.00
0766841456	Combustion Ground Rules (B / CD-ROM), 408 Pages	Peterson	1,175.00
0766828611	Construction Scheduling with Primavera Enterprise, 2/ed, 390 Pgs	Marchman	700.00
0766812405	Customizing AutoCAD 2000, 561 Pages	Tickoo	200.00
0766838528	Customizing AutoCAD 2002, 484 Pages	Tickoo	200.00
0766820084	Director 8 & Lingo (Inside Macromedia) (B / CD-ROM), 656 Pages	Wilson	800.00
076682909X	Flash 5 Graphics, Animation & Interactivity (B / CD-ROM), 642 Pages	Mohler	1,060.00
1401827551	Harnessing 3ds Max 5 (B / CD-ROM), 908 Pages	Bousquet	1,150.00
0766838463	Harnessing AutoCAD 2002 (B / CDROM), 1,215 Pages	Stellman	200.00
053868822X	HTML & JavaScript: Programming, 166 Pages	Stellman	300.00
9812542582	Java: A Framework for Program Design and DataStructures, 2/ed (B / CD-ROM), 640 Pages	Lambert	500.00
9812542590	Java Programming: Advanced Topics, 3/ed (B / 3CD-ROM), 1008 Pages	Wigglesworth	750.00
0766834700	Mastering the Art of Production with 3D Studio Max 4, (B / CD-ROM), 1,640 Pages	Bousquet	675.00
981243870X	Oracle 9i Database Administrator: Implementation & Administration, (B / CD-ROM), 562 Pages	Mccullough-Dieter	575.00
981243867X	Oracle 9i Developers: PL/SQL Programming, 560 Pages	Casteel	475.00
981243884X	Oracle 9i: SQL with An Introduction to PL/SQL, 560 Pages	Morris	550.00
0766338501	Using AutoCAD 2002 (B / CD-ROM), 1,110 Pages	Autodesk Press	200.00
0538689978	Web Page Design (All Pages in 4 Color)	Stubbs	250.00

Shroff / Wrox
(Now an imprint of John Wiley & Sons)

PUBLISHED TITLES

ISBN	Title	Author	Price
8173661146	ASP .NET Website Programming, 562 Pages	Bellinaso	400.00
8173666938	ASP .NET Website Programming: Problem-Design-Solution: VB .NET Edition, 558 Pages	Bellinaso	500.00
8173661499	Beginning Active Server Pages 3.0, 1,224 Pages	Buser	600.00
8173664781	Beginning ASP .NET 1.0 Databases using VB .NET, 482 Pages	Kauffman	375.00
8173664773	Beginning ASP .NET 1.0 with C#, 878 Pages	Goode	400.00
8173662258	Beginning ASP .NET 1.0 with VB .NET, 814 Pages	Goode	400.00
8173665559	Beginning C#, 2/ed 936 Pages	Watson	650.00
8173666423	Beginning Dynamic Websites with ASP NET Web Matrix (B / CD-ROM), 574 Pages	Sussman	575.00
8173665591	Beginning Java 2 SDK 1.4 Edition, 1,188 Pages	Horton	450.00
8173661618	Beginning JavaScript, 1,052 Pages	Wilton	300.00
8173661561	Beginning Linux Programming 2/ed, 988 Pages	Matthew	425.00
8173665052	Beginning VB .NET, 2/ed, 886 Pages	Blair	350.00
8173660409	Beginning Visual C++ 6, 1,216 Pages	Horton	600.00
8173666040	Expert One-on-One J2EE Design and Development, 768 Pages	Johnson	650.00
8173665990	Professional Apache Tomcat, 556 Pages	Chopra	500.00
8173664331	Professional ASP .NET 1.0 - Special Edition, 1,392 Pages	Anderson	500.00
8173664528	Professional C#, 2/ed, 1,262 Pages	Robinson	500.00
8173665966	Professional Crystal Reports for Visual Studio .NET, 348 Pages	McAmis	275.00
8173666334	Professional IBM WebSphere 5.0 Application Server, (B / 2 CD-ROMS), 784 Pages	Francis	650.00
8173662053	Professional SQL Server 2000 DTS (Data Transformation Services), 888 Pages	Chaffin	625.00
8173662061	Professional SQL Server 2000 Programming, 1,428 Pages	Vieira	850.00
8173666083	Professional UML with Visual Studio .NET, 364 Pages	Filev	350.00
8173664722	Professional VB .NET, 2/ed, 1,020 Pages	Barwell	450.00
817366224X	VBScript Programmer's Reference, 444 Pages	Clark	350.00
8173662223	XSLT Programmer's Reference, 2/ed, 984 Pages	Kay	275.00

Other Computer Titles

ISBN	Title	Author	Price
8173660034	AS/400 Architecture & Applications, 332 Pages	Lawrence	250.00
8173660042	AS/400: A Practical Guide to Programming & Operations, 284 Pages	Zeilenga	225.00
8173660018	CICS: A How-To for Cobol Programmers, 428 Pages	Kirk	300.00

ISBN	Title	Author	Price
0130851353	Enterprise Application Integration with XML & Java (B I CD-ROM), 469 Pages	Morgenthal	450.00
8173660026	MVS / VSAM for the Application Programmer, 504 Pages	Brown	325.00
8173660077	TCP/IP Companion: A Guide For The Common User, 284 Pages	Arick	225.00
8173660425	Vijay Mukhi's ERP Odyssey: Implementing. PeopleSoft Financials 7.0/7.5, 528 Pages	Mukhi	350.00

V.K. Publishers

ISBN	Title	Author	Price
8190133152	Database Programming Using VB .NET & SQL Server 2000, 472 Pages	Krishna	350.00
8190133101	Develop An Accounting Package Using Visual Basic & ADO, 372 Pages	Krishna	350.00
8190133128	Develop An Inventory Management Application Using Microsoft Visual Basic, 374 Pages	Krishna	345.00

- Dates & Prices of forthcoming titles are tentative and subject to change without notice.
- All Prices are in Indian Rupees except where indicated in € (Euro Dollar) $ (US Dollar) and £ (Pound)
- TITLES RELEASED AFTER FEBRUARY 2005 ARE MARKED IN BOLD.